Benjamin Leopold Farjeon

Toilers of Babylon

Vol. 2

Benjamin Leopold Farjeon

Toilers of Babylon
Vol. 2

ISBN/EAN: 9783337244231

Printed in Europe, USA, Canada, Australia, Japan

Cover: Foto ©ninafisch / pixelio.de

More available books at **www.hansebooks.com**

TOILERS OF BABYLON

BY

B. L. FARJEON,

AUTHOR OF "BLADE-O'-GRASS," "GRIF," "THE TRAGEDY OF FEATHERSTONE,"
"IN A SILVER SEA," ETC.

For life the prologue is to death,
And love its sweetest flower;
And death is as the spring of life,
And love its richest dower.

IN THREE VOLUMES.
VOL. II.

London:
WARD AND DOWNEY,
12, YORK STREET, COVENT GARDEN, W.C.
1888.

[*All rights reserved.*]

CHARLES DICKENS AND EVANS,
CRYSTAL PALACE PRESS.

TOILERS OF BABYLON.

CHAPTER I.

When Mr. Loveday, the bookseller in Church Alley, heard of his brother's death in a letter which Nansie wrote to him, he fell to reproaching himself for the small grief he experienced at the news. The intelligence did not, indeed, create within him any profound impression. He and his brother had been separated for a great many years, and the bond of love which had united them in their childhood had become weaker and weaker till it scarcely held together. It is true that death strengthened it somewhat, but it could never again be what it once was.

The humanly selfish cares of life are so engrossing that love which is not in evidence dies gradually away. That "absence makes the heart grow fonder" is as false as are nine out of ten of other sentimental proverbs.

"Timothy," said Mr. Loveday to his new assistant, who was proving himself a perfect treasure, "when little Teddy died you were very sorry."

"I was more than sorry, sir," said Timothy, becoming instantly grave; "I was almost heart-broken."

"Have you got over it?" asked Mr. Loveday.

"I shall never get over it," replied Timothy.

"Do you think that will be true all your life long?"

"I am certain it will be, sir."

"And yet you were not related to him."

"No, sir; but I could not have loved a brother more."

Mr. Loveday winced.

"You regard that as a very strong tie, Timothy."

"A brother's love, sir?"

"Yes."

"I can hardly imagine a stronger. If I had a brother I should so love him that I think I should be ready to die for him."

"Ah!" mused Mr. Loveday, "perhaps, if my brother had died when we were boys together, I should not be reproaching myself now for not feeling his death more keenly."

As a penance, he inflicted a punishment upon himself. Since he had taken Timothy into his service his life had been easier and more agreeable than it had been for a considerable time past. He was no longer tormented by small worries, which, after a long recurrence of them, become, in certain stages of mental irritation, veritable mountains of evil. Timothy had more than one rare gift, and not one more precious and beneficial in its effect upon others than the gift of thoughtfulness. This, extending to the most trivial matter where his own interests were not involved, was invariably displayed by Timothy when opportunity offered, and it was natural, therefore, that in his new and important position in Mr. Loveday's business and household, it should come into play with greater force. The result was that not a day passed without Mr. Loveday being made aware that he had enlisted in his service a lad who seemed bent upon making everything go on smoothly around him. Heaven only knows where Timothy picked up all he knew; it was likely the outcome of a willing, cheerful, practical spirit, and of one who knew how to profit by observation; but Timothy, who had never learnt how to cook, could cook a chop and a steak and a potato to perfection, and before long could prepare more ambitious dishes in a manner to satisfy his master's not very fastidious taste; and Timothy, who had never passed an apprenticeship in domestic service, could and did apply himself with skilful efficiency to the thousand and one drudgeries of domestic affairs. Moreover, he did his work neatly and unobtrusively. There were no sudden noises now in Mr. Loveday's establishment; no unreasonable breakages of crockery; and, what Mr. Loveday thoroughly appreciated, no waste. It could not be but that Mr. Loveday noted with gratefulness this improvement in his surroundings, and therefore, being at ease and in rare peace of mind, the punishment he inflicted upon himself for not taking the news of his brother's death more closely to heart was really no light one. It was to write to Nansie and remind her, if she needed reminding, that he had promised her father to give her the shelter of his home.

"My dear Niece" (he wrote)—"The

intelligence you have conveyed to me of your dear father's death has deeply affected me——"

He broke off here and sat, pen in hand, ruminating, with his eyes fixed upon the words he had written. "I suppose," he thought, "that life could not be carried on without duplicity. Here am I, for the purpose of self-defence, where I am not openly accused, and of proving that I am not quite a monster, calmly presenting myself in a false light to a young person whom I saw only once in my life and do not in the least remember. But what kind of a world would this be, I wonder, if the exact truth were always told?"

He continued his letter:

"I knew that he was ill, but had no idea he was in a dangerous state, or I should not have neglected coming to see him. However, there is no recalling the past, and regrets, though poignant, are idle in a case like this, where the blow that has fallen is irremediable. I do not intend to reproach you for your neglect of a duty, which very likely, because of our being comparative strangers, did not present itself to you in such a light, but I feel strongly the loss of the opportunity of attending my dear brother's funeral. Had you written to me when he died I certainly should have come down to you, and have done whatever lay in my power to soften your affliction."

He broke off again and mused. "'Words, words, words,' as Hamlet says. And yet I could almost deceive myself by believing that they are true. I *should* have gone down, and perhaps with something of the full heart which I am endeavouring to express to my niece Nansie. It is a curious way of spelling the name, but I like it better than Nancy. It is more poetical; but there was always a vein of poetry in my brother's nature." The tenderness in him was growing stronger, and he found comfort in it as he plied his pen again.

"I will not ask you why you were silent. You doubtless had your reasons, one of which, perhaps, was that you were doubtful of me, and that you regarded me as little better than a stranger. In this you are not to blame, but if such a feeling exists I desire to remove it. Some little while ago your father wrote to me of his circumstances, and of his anxiety respecting you in the event of anything happening to him. In my reply, I told him that you could always find a home with me. From imperfect knowledge I gather that my dear brother left but little worldly wealth behind him; and my principal object in writing to you now is to convey to you the offer of my home which I made to him. Whether we should suit each other remains to be seen, but I would endeavour honestly to be kind to you, and if you inherit any of your father's amiable qualities, I have no doubt that we should get along comfortably together. I have no ties of women and children about me; my home is a poor one, but such as it is, it is yours if you choose to accept it."

This was the gist of Mr. Loveday's letter to Nansie, who read it with satisfaction. When it arrived Kingsley was absent, winding up his affairs, and the first thing Nansie did upon his return was to give it to him to read.

"Did you tell him you were married?" asked Kingsley.

"No," replied Nansie. "To tell you the truth, Kingsley, I scarcely know in what light to regard him."

"He says something to that effect in his letter," remarked Kingsley, "but it seems to be honestly and sincerely written."

"I think so, too," said Nansie.

"But you see," said Kingsley, "in his

offer of a home—which is very kind; I do not underrate it—he evidently looks upon you as a single young lady."

"I shall write, telling him that I am married."

"It will be best; and write soon, else he might think there was something wrong —of which, my dear," added Kingsley, rubbing his forehead, "I am not quite sure myself."

"What makes you say that, Kingsley?" asked Nansie, anxiously.

"Well, my darling," replied Kingsley, "it is altogether the best to look things straight in the face, isn't it?"

"Quite the best, dear."

"We have decided on that before, Nansie."

"Yes, dear."

"It isn't the first time I have made the remark, but that does not lessen its force and truth. Well, then, my affairs are settled."

"Is everything paid, Kingsley?"

"Everything. We do not owe one penny in the world. What do you think I discovered, Nansie?"

"I cannot imagine, dear."

"That I had a great deal more property than I supposed."

"That is delightful news, dear."

"Yes, isn't it?" said Kingsley, with a light, puzzled laugh. "When I say property, I don't mean land. Wish I *could* mean it, because it would represent something tangible in the way of an income, perhaps; and that is what we want, Nansie, don't we? An income."

"It would be very pleasant, dear," said Nansie, with a fond look of pity at him.

"Yes, very pleasant; it would rub away the crosses of life."

She recalled him to his theme.

"You were saying that you discovered you had more property than you supposed?"

"Yes, that is what I was saying. And not land, as I should have liked; but wine. Really a little stock, and of the best. Of course it would be the best. And books, some of them valuable; and bric-à-brac. I was astonished when we came to look through them. And pictures, too. I was surprised how ever I came to buy them; but money always burnt in my pockets, Nansie. When it was there it had to be spent. Do you know a greater pleasure, my dear, than spending money?"

"It is a pleasant occupation, Kingsley, when one has it to spare."

"Of course, that."

"Do me a great favour, dear."

"I will. Just say what it is."

"Tell me everything you did while you were away, without—without——"

Kingsley laughed gaily and took up her words.

"Without flying off into side paths, eh?

Keep to the main road. Is that the great favour ?"

" Yes, dear."

" Very good. I will try. But just consider, Nansie—only for a moment; I will not detain you longer than a moment. Here we are, you and I—the best company in the world, my darling—walking along the main road. Very grand, very stately, very wide. Everything according to regulation. It is a very long road—it generally is, Nansie—and there is an overpowering sameness about it. My feeling is that it is becoming tiresome, when all at once I see, on the left or the right, a little narrow lane with a hedge on each side; at the end of the hedge, some cottages, dotted here and there, with flowers in the windows; at the end of the cottages some tall trees, meeting and forming an arch. What do we do? Without thinking, we turn from the grand main road into the little narrow lane, and the moment we do so we breathe more freely and begin to enjoy. That is an illustration of my manner, dear. Do you recognise it?"

"Yes, dear Kingsley."

"It isn't unpleasant, is it? Confess, now."

"Nothing that you do, dear, can be unpleasant. But remember what you said a few days ago. We must be practical."

Nansie did not utter these words in a serious tone. On the contrary, her voice was almost as light as Kingsley's, and as she spoke she laid her hand upon his shoulder, and smiled with bright affection. He kissed her, and replied with animation and decision:

"Exactly. That is what we are going to be. So now for the great favour. Well, I commenced by going through my property and being surprised. Then I went to the tradesmen to whom I owed money, and said: 'Make out your bills and send them in.'

One or two inquired whether I was going to pay. I said, 'Of course—what else?' When they heard that—I refer to those who, to my astonishment, appeared a little uneasy about the money I owed them—they said, 'Oh, but there's no hurry, Mr. Manners. We will send in the account at the end of the year.' But I said, 'No; at once, if you please.' When they came in I did not examine them; I laid them carefully aside in their envelopes. Then I went to an auctioneer, and gave him instructions to sell all my property. I wished him to do it immediately—that very day, but he would not; he said it would involve too great a sacrifice; but that was my affair, not his. It is unaccountable that people will *not* do the thing you want done in your way, but in their own. However, I hurried my friend the auctioneer as much as I could, and the result of it all was, that I found myself two hundred pounds richer than I had supposed."

"How pleased I am, Kingsley!"

"So was I. It seemed to me as if I had discovered a gold mine. Then I sat down with a clean sheet of ruled foolscap before me, and opened the tradesmen's accounts, and put down the figures, and totted them up. The result was that I found I owed four hundred pounds more than I had supposed."

"Oh, Kingsley!"

"It was vexing, but there it was, and there was no help for it. I went about my affairs in the practical way, did I not?"

"Yes, my dear; it was the only way to arrive at the truth."

"And to look it straight in the face. I kept to the main road, but if a view of a narrow lane had presented itself, I believe I should have been tempted to wander a little. My dear, I paid all the accounts, and I was left with — how much do you think?"

"I am afraid to guess, Kingsley."

"Something under ten pounds. Was I dashed? Did I despair? Not at all. Said I to myself, said I—by the way, Nansie, I once came across an old novel with just that title; an odd one, isn't it?—said I to myself, said I, to work, to work! Something must be done, for my dear Nansie's sake."

"How proud I am of you, Kingsley!"

"Thank you, dear. So what did I do? I can sketch a little in colours, you know."

"You can paint very well, Kingsley. When you said, the other night, that you saw pictures but could not paint them, I knew you were wrong, though I did not contradict you."

"Thank you again, dear. Nothing would please me better than to be a poor artist, with you, rich and influential, for my patron."

"I should give you every shilling I possessed, Kingsley."

"And you call yourself practical. Nonsense, nonsense! It is I who am the practical one. I proved it. I bought water-colours, drawing-paper, pencils, brushes, a nice little outfit for thirty-eight shillings, and, Nansie, I set to work. Upon my honour, I painted a picture which I considered not bad."

"What did you do with it? You have brought it with you?"

"No, my dear little wife, I sold it."

"Why, Kingsley," said Nansie, in a delighted tone, "you have actually already made a start."

"I have," said Kingsley, laughing heartily. "The picture painted, I took it out to the shops. My dear, they rather pooh-poohed it at first."

"They ought to have been ashamed of themselves," exclaimed Nansie, indignantly.

"They weren't. But I met with a patron at last. He was a stationer, and said the picture was of no use to him. 'But it's worth something,' I said. To be honest with you, Nansie, I was getting rather disgusted with the whole affair. 'It's worth something,' I said. 'Two-pence,' said the shopkeeper. 'Done,' said I, and I threw the picture on the counter, and held out my hand. He stared at me, but I gave him to understand that he had offered me two-pence for my picture, and that I accepted it. He stared harder than ever and handed me the two-pence. It is the first money I ever earnt in my life, and I have brought it home to you. The experiment was a capital one, Nansie; it taught me something — that I am not cut out for a painter. Next to discovering what you can do, the best thing is to discover what you can't do. Having discovered it, turn the key on it."

Nansie gazed at him sadly. He was speaking with animation, and there was an excited flush in his face. His eyes were bright, and his manner was indicative of anything but disappointment.

"I thought then," continued Kingsley, "that I would try my friends, but when I came to consider, I arrived at the conclusion that there was only one to whom I could disclose my position. I went to him and made full confession. He is an older fellow than I, and wiser. What I like about him is that he doesn't say: 'You shouldn't have done this,' or 'You shouldn't have done that.' He hits the nail on the head. 'There is no hope of your father relenting?' said he. 'None,' said I. 'Time may soften him,' he said. 'Even if it does,' said I, 'there is a problem to solve while the grass is growing.' 'You must live,' said he, 'of course.' 'Of course,' said I. 'And you must work to live,' said he. I assented. 'Then,' said he, 'let us see what you are fit for.' My own thought, Nansie, put almost in my own words. But although we considered and talked we arrived at nothing tangible. He seemed really more troubled than I was, and at the end of a long conversation he said: 'Kingsley, old fellow, I can lend you a tenner.' It was noble of him, because he must have known that there was little chance of my being able to repay him. I thanked him, and said I wouldn't borrow in such circumstances as mine. Then he invited me to dine with him, and I accepted. And that, my dear Nansie, is all I have to tell you."

He gazed round at Nansie with the air of a man who had just finished a pleasant tale, and said:

"Now we will talk of something else."

CHAPTER II.

NANSIE wrote to her uncle before she went to bed, informing him that she was married, and thanking him for the kind letter he had sent her. She said nothing as to the offer of a home, because she did not consider that it held good. Nansie single and Nansie married could not bear the same relation in her uncle's eyes. Single, she needed a protector; married, she possessed one. The responsibility of affairs lay with her husband; all that it was in her power to do was to wait and see what steps he took towards providing for their home. She could encourage and strengthen him, but for the present that was all. To attempt so early to assume the direction of affairs would have been an affront to her husband's manhood, and as, out of loyalty to Kingsley, she purposely avoided the contemplation of this contingency, she had no idea what steps it would be advisable for her to take in the event of Kingsley's failure.

On the following morning she told Kingsley that she had written to her uncle, and asked him if he would like to read the letter before it was posted. Kingsley replied that as she must have written about him he would prefer not to see it.

"I have written everything that is good about you," she said.

"That is the reason," said Kingsley. "My dear, I trust you implicitly, and I am satisfied that you have said exactly what is right—with one exception. You have spoken too highly of your husband. Don't shake your head, I know it. You have an exaggerated opinion of me, or, to phrase it better, you have formed an ideal which will not bear the test of sober truth. But that, dear little wife, is the fate of most ideals."

"What you say," observed Nansie, "will apply with equal truth to your opinion of me."

"Not at all," said Kingsley, with fond seriousness, "you stand away and apart from me—higher, nobler, more capable. I will not listen to any contradiction, my dear, when I am discussing *you*. The fact is, I have already applied the test."

"In what way, Kingsley?" asked Nansie.

She was learning that it was best to humour him in certain moods, which it seemed impossible for him to avoid.

"In this. Of course, when I first saw you I formed my ideal of you. What it was, I think you know to some small extent, for the love I feel and express for you is no idle sentiment. Whatever else I may be, I am at least as true as steel to you. It is one virtue

I may fairly claim, for nothing which is inspired by you can be anything else. Well, knowing you but slightly, my ideal was formed, and familiar association would either destroy or establish it. My dear, I have questioned myself, I have asked: 'Does Nansie come up to your ideal? Is she the true woman you supposed her to be? Does she represent what you believed—the sweetness, the purity, the nobility, the tenderness which have sanctified the very name of woman?' The answer is: 'She is all, and more than all, you believed her to be. There is nothing in her that is not sweet, and true, and good. The ideal you set up falls short of the reality.' Then, on the other hand, is the question of Me. I do not wish to disturb you, my dear, but I fear a terrible disappointment awaits you when you have found me out. No, I will not allow you to answer me. You may stand up in my defence when I am not present, but my imperfections are too apparent—now that I am brought face to face with them—to encourage any attempt to smooth them away. However, we are bound to each other for better or worse, and you must make the best of me. Now address your letter to your uncle, and I will post it for you."

"Shall I give him your love, Kingsley?" asked Nansie, adding hurriedly, "you are very unjust to yourself."

"Yes, dear, give him my love, and say that I hope to make his acquaintance one day. As to being unjust to myself, I know I am the best judge of that."

He went from the room, and in a few minutes presented himself again, gloved and polished, a faithful presentment of a young English gentleman.

"You must wish me luck, Nansie," he said. "I am going to see what can be done in the way of obtaining a situation. Perhaps something fortunate will turn up."

She kissed him and watched him from the street door walking along the street, looking brightly this way and that for something to turn up. He returned at six o'clock in the evening, in time for dinner. There was a jaded expression on his face, which vanished the moment his eyes rested on Nansie.

"Home, sweet home," he said, passing his arms round her waist, and drinking in her beauty with a grateful spirit.

She knew that he had not been successful in his quest, but nevertheless she asked what fortune he had met with.

"None at all," he replied; "but Rome wasn't built in a day. We must have patience. I will tell you after dinner what I have done."

They had the pleasantest of meals, enlivened by his gaiety; and when the things were cleared away and he had lit his cigar, he said:

"What can a man wish for more? A

good dinner, the sweetest of company, a fine cigar—it was right, was it not, Nansie, for me to keep back three hundred of my choicest?"

"Quite right," replied Nansie, "and very thoughtful of you. I love the smell of a good cigar."

"When I put them aside," said Kingsley, holding up a reproving fore-finger, "I thought only of myself. I reflected that it might be some time before I could afford to buy more of the same kind."

"Kingsley," said Nansie, pleadingly.

"Yes, dear," he responded.

"I want you to understand something."

"Anything you wish, Nansie. Let me know what it is."

"Only that your disparagement of yourself hurts me, dear. Knowing that there is nothing in the world you would not do for my sake, it is painful to me to think that you may grow into the habit of believing that everything you do is done with a selfish motive. It is not so—indeed it is not so!"

"How seriously you speak, Nansie!" said Kingsley, drawing her close to him. "Do you really mean to say that I am not selfish?"

"If there is in the world a man who has proved himself otherwise, it is you, my dear," said Nansie, laying her head upon his shoulder. "Be just to yourself, in justification of me."

"That requires elucidation, my dearest," said Kingsley, with great tenderness.

"Think of the sacrifice you have made for me, a poor girl, but for whom you would be now at peace with your parents, and in the enjoyment of much, if not of all, that makes life worth living. How low should I fall in your estimation if I were insensible to that sacrifice, if I were to undervalue it, if I were to say: 'It is what any other man in Kingsley's place would have done!'"

"Is it not?" he asked, passing his hand fondly over her hair.

"No, indeed and indeed it is not. I do not pretend to assert that I know the world as you know it"—there was something whimsical in the expression of unconsciously-affected wisdom which stole into Kingsley's face as she uttered these words—"but I know it sufficiently well to be certain that there are few men capable of a sacrifice such as you have made for me. What had I to give in return?"

"Love," he answered.

"It is yours," she said, and tears, in which there was no unhappiness, stole into her eyes, "love as perfect as woman ever gave to man. Not love for to-day, my dearest, but love for ever; love which nothing can weaken; love which will triumph over every adversity; love which will be proof against any trial. But that is little."

"It is everything," said Kingsley, "to me and to every man worthy of the name. The sacrifice I have made—you choose to call it so, and I will not contradict you, dear—is to be measured. Not so with love. It is illimitable, unmeasurable. It illumines every surrounding object; it makes the commonest things precious. How beautiful the present is to you and to me! Could it be more beautiful if we were passing it in a palace? That picture on the wall—a common print? No. A lovely possession. The handsomest painting that ever was painted hanging there —would it make the present moments sweeter, would it invest the spiritual bond which unites us with a binding link which now is missing? This book on the table which cost a shilling—if it were a first edition worth thousands of pounds, would it increase our happiness, would it make your love for me and mine for you more perfect and complete? There is an immeasurable distance between what I have gained and what I have lost. So let us have no more talk of sacrifices, Nansie, dear."

She could not find arguments with which to answer him, and it would have been strange if she had needed them.

"In return," he continued, "I will make the strongest endeavour not to underrate myself, nor to prove that I am more than ordinarily selfish. There—my cigar is out."

She lit a match and held it while he puffed away at his weed.

"You promised to tell me what you have done to-day," she said.

"There is very little to tell. I did what I could, which consisted simply of walking about, and looking in shop-windows. I went out without any distinct idea in my mind; I thought that something might happen, and I was disappointed. Everything and everybody seemed to be going along nicely, and not to be in want of me. It occurred to me to consider what I was fit for. I looked into the windows of a boot-shop. What do I know of boots and shoes, except how to put them on my feet? Literally nothing. The same with haberdashers, the same with grocers, the same with jewellers, the same with every kind of shop. Then, trades; I don't know one. Printers, engravers, carpenters, watchmakers, and that kind of thing—you have to serve an apprenticeship before you can hope to earn money by them. I felt like a fish out of water. There seemed to be no groove for me, nothing that I could take hold of. I am really puzzled, Nansie."

"My poor Kingsley!" murmured Nansie.

"But, there," he said, snapping his fingers, "it will not mend matters to worry about them. *Nil desperandum*, and a fig for the world and its cares! If only to-morrow would not come!"

He certainly had the gift of giving dull care the go-by; and in another minute he was the same light-hearted, pleasant-humoured, irresponsible being he had ever been, and was doing his best with his whimsical talk to make Nansie forget the serious position in which they were placed.

CHAPTER III.

SOME indication has been given of the success of Timothy Chance's service with Mr. Loveday. There are men, like Kingsley Manners, who, being suddenly thrust upon the world to shift for themselves, find themselves plunged into a sea of difficulties, extrication from which is impossible except by some unexpected windfall of fortune. There are others who are so well armed for difficulties, that the encountering of them serves as an incentive and a spur. What depresses one elevates the other; what makes one despondent makes the other cheerful. It is chiefly a matter of early education, in which adversity is frequently a factor for good.

Partly, also, it is a matter of adaptability.

It may be taken for granted that wherever Timothy Chance fell he would fall upon his feet, and that he would be among the first to take advantage of an opportunity. A hard-working, faithful servant, but with an eye to his own interests. It is running far ahead of events to state that, when he was a middle-aged man, with a house of his own, there stood upon a bracket in his private room the image of a hen fashioned in gold—a valuable ornament; for the gold was of the purest, and the bird was of life-size; and that the sense of possession imparted a satisfaction to Timothy Chance far beyond its value. He amused himself by the fancy that the fowl of gold was an exact reproduction of the living fowl which he had rescued from the fire in the school-house, and which had laid an egg in Mr. Loveday's shop on the day of Timothy's return to

London. The goose of the fable that laid golden eggs was an insignificant bird in comparison with Timothy Chance's first fowl. There was at first a difficulty respecting its habitation. Mr. Loveday's shop had no backyard, and for the sake of cleanliness it could not be kept in the house. There were, however, plenty of backyards in the immediate vicinity of Church Alley, and to the proprietor of one of these Timothy betook himself, arranging to pay rent in kind, that is to say (for we are approaching legal ground) one new-laid egg per week, or in default, its full retail value, seven farthings. For it was not long before Timothy discovered that he could dispose of a limited number of new-laid eggs—the day of laying being guaranteed—to private persons at that rate per egg. Timothy's hen was certainly a wonderful layer; during the first thirty-one days of its tenancy of the Whitechapel backyard, it laid no fewer than twenty-six eggs, which, deducting five for rental, left twenty-one to the good. A retired butterman, who should undoubtedly have been a good judge, engaged to take them all at the price above mentioned, and at the end of the month the account stood thus:

	s.	d.
21 rent-paid eggs at 1¾d.	3	0¾
Less, food for fowl, at the rate of ½d. per day	1	3½
Leaving a net profit of	1	9¼

This is a precise copy of the account made out by Timothy Chance, on the termination of the month; and with the figures, clear and well-shaped before him, Timothy devoted himself to thought. His service with the seller of second-hand books had served him in good stead. He had rummaged out from among the stock at least a score of books treating of fowls and their produce, and he had studied them attentively. Some were old, one or two were of late years, and they all pointed to one fact — that money was to be made out of eggs. Most of the writers deplored the fact that the English people were so blind to their own interests as to systematically neglect a subject so fruitful. One of the treatises dealt in large figures—to wit, the population of Great Britain, and the number of eggs by them consumed annually; further, the number of eggs laid in the kingdom, and the number we were compelled to import to satisfy the demand, amounting not to scores but to hundreds of millions. Timothy's eyes dilated. One daring enthusiast went so far as to print pages of statistics to prove that if Government took the affair in hand, it could, in a certain number of years (number forgotten by the present chronicler), pay off the national debt. This, perhaps, was too extravagant, but the fact remained, and appeared incontrovertible, that money was to be made out of eggs. Here was plain proof—one shilling and ninepence farthing made out of one hen in a single month.

"Let me see," mused Timothy, "how this turns out for the year."

Down went the figures.

	s.	d.
Cost of food, 365 days at ½d. per day	15	2½
Cost of fowl, say	3	0
	18	2½

For a moment he forgot the rent, but he remembered it before he went into the credit side, and he reckoned it at a penny a week, which made the total expenses £1 2s. 6½d.

Timothy was aware that he could not reckon upon an egg a day all through the year, but his reading up on the subject, and the calculations he had made, convinced him that a fair-laying hen might be depended upon for two hundred and forty eggs during the three hundred and sixty-five days.

"At three-halfpence each," he mused, and set down the figures, "that will bring in thirty shillings. Say it brings in only twenty-eight shillings, and make the total charges one pound four, and there remains a clear profit of four shillings for the year. Then the fowl itself, supposing I sell it at the end of the year, is worth at least a shilling. A profit of five shillings on one hen. On twenty, a profit of five pounds; on a hundred, a profit of twenty-five pounds; on a thousand, a profit of two hundred and fifty pounds."

The figures almost took his breath away. Let it be understood that Timothy's reflections and calculations are here pretty accurately reported. He continued. So large a number of eggs would have to be sold wholesale, and three-halfpence each could not be reckoned upon, but then the rent would be much less, and the cost of food much less; and there were other ideas floating in his mind which he could not formulate, and about which there was no cause for his troubling himself just at present.

"Mr. Loveday," said he to his employer, "if a speculation is entered into in a small way and leaves a small profit, would it not leave a larger profit if entered into in a large way?"

"That," replied Mr. Loveday, "stands to reason. What is your head running on, Timothy?"

"Eggs, sir," said Timothy.

Mr. Loveday stared at him for a few moments without speaking.

"That is what you have been studying books on poultry for?" he said, presently.

"Yes, sir."

"Well," said Mr. Loveday, after another pause, "there's something in eggs, I dare say. Some of the peasantry in France make quite an income out of them; our own poor country-folk are not so far-seeing."

"What can be done in France," said Timothy, patriotically and sententiously, "can be done in England."

"Don't be too certain of that," said Mr. Loveday. "They grow grapes in France and make wine. We don't."

"That is a matter of climate," remarked Timothy. "Fowls lay eggs in every country in the world, and once laid, there they are."

"To be sure," said Mr. Loveday, staring at his assistant, "there they are."

"Anyhow," said Timothy, "nothing can alter that what will pay in a small way ought to pay in a large, can it, sir?"

"The conclusion appears sensible and reasonable. I suppose you have made something out of your fowl."

"Nearly two shillings in the month, sir."

"Not at all bad," said Mr. Loveday, "not at all bad. You must take the breed into account."

"Black Hamburgs, sir, that's the breed for eggs."

"Dorkings, I should say," suggested Mr. Loveday.

"Black Hamburgs will beat them, sir," said Timothy, confidently; and Mr. Loveday, feeling that he was on unsafe ground, wisely held his tongue.

Timothy had saved between five and six shillings out of his wages, and he expended the whole of his savings in putting up a rough fowl-house, and in the addition of a black Hamburg to his live stock. He began to feel like a proprietor.

"Slow and sure, you know, Timothy," advised Mr. Loveday.

"Yes, sir, and thank you," said Timothy. "I will endeavour not to make mistakes."

"We shall have you Chancellor of the Exchequer in course of time," said Mr. Loveday, in a tone by no means unkindly.

"I shall be content to earn a living, sir," said Timothy, modestly; and rejoiced largely when he showed his employer two new-laid eggs in one day.

CHAPTER IV.

THREE months after this conversation Mr. Loveday and Timothy were standing in front of the book-shop, discussing some proposed alterations in the stall outside upon which the more promiscuous books were offered for sale. The weather was fine, and a bright sun was striving to make its presence known in Church Alley; a bird in a cage hung above Mr. Sly's shop window was piping a song of gratitude and welcome, and a cat, caught by a sunbeam, stood stock still enjoying the warmth. A young woman, neatly and plainly dressed, entered Church Alley, and with timid, hesitating steps, gazed at the shops and houses as she passed them, halting within a yard of the stall before which Mr. Loveday and Timothy were talking. Timothy was explaining his views. The new stall could be made with flaps, hanging down, which, when rain threatened, could be swiftly raised to enclose the books. This would do away with the old and cumbersome method of covering the outside stock with canvas.

"And besides, sir, it could be made to fit like a box, with a good padlock outside, so that there would be no need to take the books out and in morning and night. The expense would not be great, only the timber. I can borrow tools, and make it as well as a carpenter. I don't mind saying that a thorough good workman couldn't beat my fowl-house."

"There's nothing much you can't do, Timothy," said Mr. Loveday.

"These things are not difficult, sir, if one only puts one's mind to them. A good saw and plane, a chisel, a few nails and hinges, and it is done."

"You shall try your hand, Timothy," said Mr. Loveday, and turned to go into his shop.

As he did so, his eyes rested upon the figure of the young woman who had halted within a few steps of him.

He was transfixed. Twenty and odd years of his life were suddenly engulphed in a memory of the past.

There stood the woman he had loved and lost—the woman whom his dead brother had loved and married.

He stood like a man in a dream, or under a spell of enchantment. All consciousness of the present time had vanished. The past came back again, the love which had slept so long that he had deemed it dead awoke within him and stirred his heart. Was it joy, was it pain he felt as he stretched forth a trembling hand?

As if in response to that movement on his part, the woman moved towards him, and held out her two hands with an affectionate look in her eyes, in which there dwelt also some touch of entreaty.

"Who are you?" he asked, faintly, recovering his voice.

"I am Nansie," was the reply. "I recognised you, uncle, by your likeness to my dear father."

"And I recognised you," he said, "by your likeness to your dear mother. How like you are to her—how like, how like!"

"I am glad," said Nansie. "My dear father always said I was growing to resemble her more and more. Uncle, am I welcome?"

"Quite welcome. Come in."

He was himself once more; and he took her hands in his, and conducted her into his shop.

Timothy gazed at Nansie with worshipping eyes as she passed from the open, and stood gazing—for how long he knew not—until he was aroused by Mr. Loveday suddenly appearing from the shop, and calling out to him, in an agitated tone, to run for a doctor.

"No, no," cried Nansie's voice from within, "I do not need a doctor. I only fainted a moment, I was so tired. You don't know the ways of women, uncle."

"How should I," he said, rejoining her, "having so small an acquaintance with them?"

"But you said I was welcome, uncle?" she said in a solicitous tone.

"And you are."

"You are glad to see me?"

"Yes. Why have I not seen you before? Why have I not heard from you?"

"I wrote to you, uncle."

"Telling me you were married. Yes, I forgot."

"You did not reply."

"I saw no occasion. I thought if you

wanted me you would write again, or come."

"Here I am, as you see, uncle."

"I see. Wanting me?"

"I—I think so, uncle. You shall judge."

"You speak in a voice of doubt. Listen to me, Nansie. I may call you so?"

"Surely, surely. It gives me pleasure."

"Listen, then. If there is anything in my voice or manner to cause you uneasiness, account for it by the fact that I know little of women, as you yourself said. It is sometimes my way—not always, and seldom unless I am somewhat shaken. If you had informed me that you were coming I should have been prepared. I should not then have thought, when my eyes fell upon you, that it was your mother I was gazing upon, and not her daughter."

"I am sorry," murmured Nansie.

"There is nothing to be sorry for. These reminders do a man — especially a recluse like myself — no harm. You are turning white. Are you going to faint again?"

"No; I will not allow myself."

"I have some brandy in the house. Shall I give you a little? It is a medicine."

"No, thank you, uncle; I never touch it."

"What is it, then, that makes you so white? Stay. A cup of tea?"

"If you please, uncle."

"I am a dunderhead. Timothy!"

No *genii* in Eastern tales ever appeared more promptly at a summons.

"Yes, sir."

"Make some tea; the best—quick!"

Timothy glanced at Nansie, nodded, and vanished.

"That is my assistant," said Mr. Loveday; "a treasure. A man, a boy, a girl, a woman, rolled into one. He can sew on buttons."

Nansie laughed, and Mr. Loveday gasped.

"Don't mind me," he said in explanation. "Your laugh is so like your mother's. You see, Nansie, until I grow more accustomed to you, I shall find myself driven into the past."

There was a deep tenderness in his voice, and she took his hand in hers.

"Uncle, will you not kiss me?"

He kissed her, and the tears came into his eyes.

"There," he muttered, "you see how it is. That is the first time my lips have touched a woman's face since I was a youngster. Don't think the better of me for it. What is the time? Four o'clock. Have you had dinner?"

"No, uncle."

"Lunch?"

"No, uncle."

"Breakfast?"

"Yes."

"At what hour?"

"Eight o'clock."

"And nothing since?"

"Nothing. I was so anxious to get to you, and I have been so long finding you."

"No wonder you are white and faint. Ah, there is Timothy, in my little room where we eat—and talk, I was about to say; but we talk everywhere. Come along."

There was not only tea on the table, there was a chop, beautifully cooked, and bread and butter, on a clean white cloth.

"What did I tell you of him?" said Mr. Loveday, when Timothy, after looking at the table to see that nothing was wanting, had departed. "He knew what I did not. I never met another like him. Now, eat. Ah, the colour is coming back into your face. Have you come from the country?"

"Yes, uncle."

"What station did you stop at?"

"Waterloo."

"At what time?"

"One o'clock."

"And you have been three hours getting here. Why did you not ride? I beg your pardon. No money, perhaps?"

"Oh, yes." She produced her purse, which, before she could prevent him, her uncle took from her hand.

"Two shillings and eightpence. Is it all you have?"

Her lips quivered.

"Of course you could not ride. There is no return ticket to—to the place you came from."

"I was not sure of returning there, uncle."

"Ah! I have something to hear. Or perhaps you did not have money enough to pay for a double fare. Why, Nansie, I might have been dead, for all you knew! You trusted to a slender chance. What would have happened if you had not found me? Two shillings and eightpence would have kept you till to-morrow, and then——You have something of my brother's thoughtless spirit in you."

"Say rather, uncle, of your dear brother's hope and trust."

"I will say it if you like, but it will not alter the fact that you have acted rashly. But I must learn how the land lies. You have a story to tell?"

"Yes, uncle."

"If I allow you to tell it in your own way you will stumble and break down, will cry, and faint again perhaps. I put you, therefore, in the witness-box, where you are to speak the truth, the whole truth, and nothing but the truth. Are you ready?"

"Yes, uncle,"

"No evasions, no gloss; plain and unvarnished. Deceive me once, and you will find me a tough customer. First let me say that I am agreeably surprised in you. Brought up in the country I know not how, I might have expected my niece to be a raw country wench with rough manners and small education. I find, on the contrary, a lady who can read and write."

"Yes, uncle," said Nansie, with a smile, "I can do that."

"And can cipher, perhaps."

"I am not very good at figures, uncle."

"Of course not—you are a woman. But languages now. French, perhaps?"

"Yes, uncle."

"And German?"

"Yes, uncle."

"Ah, a Crichton in petticoats. Any others?"

"Those are all the languages I can speak, uncle."

"And enough too, Nansie."

"Yes, uncle."

"I must do your father the justice to say that he has furnished you well. But I suppose you can't make a pudding?"

"Yes I can, uncle."

"Better and better. I thought I was about to learn something. And, now, when your father died he did not leave a fortune behind him?"

"He died poor."

"But you were not alone and unprotected. You had a husband by your side. It occurs to me as strange that so soon before my brother's death he should have written to me in anxiety about you, and should have asked me to give you a home here in London; and you with a husband all the time!"

"My father did not know I was married."

"But you were?"

"Yes."

"Do you mean to tell me that you were secretly married?"

"It is so, uncle."

"I never heard of a secret marriage the motive for which did not spring from the man. It was your husband's wish that your marriage should be kept secret?"

"For a time only, uncle; until his father's return from abroad."

"Of course—family reasons."

"Yes."

"The usual story. What difference would it have made if you had been married with your father's consent and knowledge? There would have been less duplicity in the affair."

"Uncle, it is difficult sometimes to see how things come about. It happened as I have told you. It might not if we had consulted my dear father beforehand."

"Would he have refused his consent?"

"It is most likely."

"Ah! However careless and unmindful my brother might have been in worldly matters, he was a gentleman and a man of fine instincts. You married a man beneath you."

"You are wrong, uncle. I married a gentleman far above me."

"And yet you tell me your father would have refused his consent."

"You forget, uncle. My dear father was truly what you have described him—a man of fine instincts."

"Well?"

"We were poor; my husband's family are very wealthy."

"I am corrected. The fact would have caused my brother to act as you say, unless, indeed, the consent of your husband's parents had been previously obtained."

"It was not, uncle."

"What rash folly! I anticipate your answer. You were in love."

"Yes, uncle."

"I am beginning to get puzzled. There is a kind of tangle here. In the first letter you wrote to me you signed yourself Nansie. Nothing more. When I replied to you I addressed you in your father's name. In your second letter, acquainting me that you were married, you signed yourself Nansie Manners."

"That is my name."

"You tell me that you have married into a wealthy family, and you come to me faint and hungry, with two-and-eightpence in your purse. And I will hazard the guess that you travelled third-class."

"I did, uncle."

"Explain the anomaly."

"When my husband told his father of our marriage he discarded him and turned him from the house."

"That explains it; but it is bad, very bad. See what comes of secret marriages. Hopes shattered, old ties broken, hearts embittered, parents and children parted in anger. Had you known all this beforehand would you have married?"

"No, uncle," replied Nansie, firmly. It was the first time the question had been put to her, and she could not but answer frankly. "I would not have done Kingsley such injustice."

"Then there has been injustice—injustice all round. Kingsley, I infer, is your husband." Nansie nodded. "Have you come into association with his family?"

"I have never seen one of them, uncle."

"Where do they live?"

"Here, in London. You have heard of them, I dare say, uncle. Kingsley's father is the great contractor, Mr. Manners."

Mr. Loveday started. "Manners, the great contractor! Why, Nansie, the man is a millionaire, and famous all the world over! You have flown high, my girl."

"I knew nothing of this. Before Kingsley and I met I had never heard of Mr. Manners; and even up to the day of our marriage I had no idea that he was so wealthy and famous. Kingsley spoke of him as being rich, but nothing more; and, uncle, I was not very worldly-wise, and should have thought a man with a thousand pounds rich. I should think so now."

"You have made no effort to see your husband's father?"

"No; it would be useless. Kingsley tells me he is a man of iron will, and never swerves from a resolution he has made. There is no hope of turning him. Was it not noble conduct, uncle, on Kingsley's part to marry me, a poor girl without a penny in the world?"

"I am not at all sure, Nansie." He opened her purse and took out the few poor coins it contained. "See what it has brought you to. Better for you if your husband had a hundred a year than a father with millions which he buttons his pockets upon. It was a rash and thoughtless act you young people have done. There is no hope of turning Mr. Manners, you say. Yet you are a lady, well mannered, well spoken, well educated; and he sprang from nothing. It is well known. But it is idle to talk in this fashion. There is a stubbornness on the part of the ignorant which is worse than the pride of those who can boast of high descent. The self-made man is often the most difficult animal to deal with. Your husband could not have contemplated the cost of what he was about to do."

"He thought only of one thing, uncle—that he loved me."

"And that is to serve as a set-off against all the ills of life. I hope it may prove so. The commencement does not hold out any great promise, that's plain. And now, Nansie, tell me the rest in your own way. I have got the nut of the story, and a precious hard one it is to crack."

"When my dear father died," said Nansie, "Kingsley was in London. Mr. Manners had just returned from Russia, and it was the first opportunity Kingsley had of making him acquainted with our marriage. I think that Kingsley, out of consideration for me, has not told me everything that passed between him and his father, but I know that Mr. Manners extracted a promise from him to remain at home for a week before he decided."

"Decided upon what?" asked Mr. Loveday, abruptly.

"I do not know, uncle; Kingsley has been so worried and troubled that it would have been unkind for me to press him upon points which really matter very little. For after all, Kingsley came back to me when I called him, and is true and faithful."

"His father perhaps pressed him to desert you and break your heart. Rich as the self-made man is, he could not divorce you. And your husband consented to remain a week in his father's house to consider it! That looks ugly."

"Kingsley did nothing wrong. He hoped by remaining near his father that a favourable moment might come when he could successfully appeal to him to deal more tenderly towards us. There was also the chance of his mother's mediation."

"Ah, there is a mother. I was going to ask about her."

"Mr. Manners is master of everything and everybody. His lightest word is law. Before the week was ended Kingsley received my letter with news of my dear father's death. Where was Kingsley's place then, uncle?"

"By your side."

"He came at once, without a single hour's delay. He asked his father to release him from his promise, and as Mr. Manners would not do so, he broke it—out of love for me. This, I think, embittered Mr. Manners more strongly against us, and he turned Kingsley from the house. I hope you are beginning to do Kingsley justice, uncle."

"He seems to have acted well. But go on."

"After my father was buried, Kingsley

and I were naturally very anxious as to how we should live. Kingsley had a little property, but he owed money to tradesmen, which had to be paid. The settlement of these accounts swallowed up nearly every sovereign he possessed, and we had a hard fight before us, harder, indeed, than we imagined. I must tell you that Kingsley wrote to his parents without success. His father returned his letter without one word of acknowledgment. If I had thought I could do any good I would have gone to his mother, but I felt that it would only make matters worse, if they could be worse. What could I have expected from her but reproaches for separating her from her son? For I am the cause of that. If Kingsley had never seen me he would have been at peace with his parents, carrying out his father's desire that he should become a Member of Parliament, and take a part in public affairs. Kingsley is fitted for it, indeed he is. He talks most beautifully. And I have spoilt it all, and have ruined a great career. I would not dare to say so to Kingsley; he would never forgive me for it. He tried hard to get some sort of work to do; he went out day after day, and used to return home so sad and wearied that it almost broke my heart to see him."

"With but a little store of money," said Mr. Loveday, "such a state of affairs must soon come to an end."

"We held out as long as we could; longer, indeed, than I thought possible. We parted with many little treasures——"

"And all this time you never wrote to me!" exclaimed Mr. Loveday.

"Remember, uncle, that I *had* written to you and that you had not sent a line of congratulation upon our marriage."

"A nice thing to congratulate you upon! But I was to blame, I admit it."

"It was a delicate matter to Kingsley.

'Your uncle doesn't care to know me,' he said; and so it seemed. At length, uncle, we came to a great block, and we truly despaired. But there was a break in the clouds, uncle."

"Good."

"I am speaking of yesterday. A letter arrived for Kingsley from a friend to whom he had written, saying that a gentleman who intended to remain abroad for three or four months required a kind of secretary and companion, and that Kingsley could secure the situation if he cared for it. The gentleman was in Paris, and the letter contained a pass to Paris, dated yesterday. We had come to our last shilling, uncle, and this separation—I hope and trust not for long—was forced upon us. Kingsley managed to raise a little money, a very little, uncle, just enough to defray his expenses to Paris and to leave me a few shillings. So last evening, when we parted, it was agreed that

I should come to London to-day, and appeal to you to give me shelter till Kingsley's return. That is all, uncle. Will you?"

"Yes, Nansie," said Mr. Loveday, "I will keep the promise I made to my dead brother."

Nansie took his hand and kissed it, and then burst into tears.

CHAPTER V.

From that day a new life commenced for Mr. Loveday. It was not that there was any great improvement in the ordinary domestic arrangements of his modest establishment, because the reign of Timothy had introduced beneficial changes in this respect before Nansie was made Queen. It was more in its spiritual than its material aspect that the new life was made manifest. To have a lady moving quietly about the house, to be greeted by a smile and a kind glance whenever he turned towards her, to hear her gentle voice addressing him without invitation on his part—all this was not only new, but wonderful and delightful. Mr.

Loveday very soon discovered that Nansie was indeed a lady, and far above the worldly station to which her circumstances relegated her; it was an agreeable discovery, and he appreciated it keenly. He found himself listening with pleasure to her soft footfall on the stairs or in the rooms above, and he would even grow nervous if any length of time elapsed without evidence of her presence in the house. Perhaps Nansie's crowning virtue was her unobtrusiveness. Everything she did was done quietly, without the least fuss or noise; no slamming of doors to jar the nerves, nothing to disturb or worry.

"Where did you learn it all, Nansie?" asked Mr. Loveday.

"It is what all women do," she replied.

He did not dispute with her, although his experience was not favourable to her view. Inwardly he said: "What all women could *not* do, if they tried ever so hard.

But then Nansie had perfection for a mother." His thoughts travelled frequently now to the early days when he loved the woman who was not to become his wife, and it may be that he accepted Nansie's companionship and presence as in some sense a recompense for his youthful disappointment, a meting out of poetical justice, as it were.

Of all the hours of day and night the evening hours were the most delightful, not only to him but to Timothy, between whom and Nansie there swiftly grew a bond of sympathy and friendship. Before Nansie's appearance Mr. Loveday's house was a comfortable one to live and work in; but from the day she first set foot in it, it became a home. Neither Timothy nor Mr. Loveday could have given an intelligible explanation of the nature of the change; but they accepted it in wonder and gratitude. Everything was the same and yet not the same. There was no addition to the furniture; but it appeared to be altogether different furniture from that to which they had been accustomed. It was brighter, cleaner, and in its new and improved arrangement acquired a new value. There were now white curtains to the windows, and the windows themselves were not coated with dust. The fireplaces were always trim and well brushed up, the fires bright and twinkling, the candlesticks and all the metal-work smartly polished, the table-linen white and clean, clothes with never a button missing, socks and stockings with never a hole in them. Nansie could have accomplished all these things unaided; but Timothy was so anxious to be employed that she would not pain him by refusing his assistance. She had another reason—a reason which she did not disclose, and which Mr. Loveday and Timothy were too inexperienced to suspect — for accepting the lad's willing service. She knew that a time was approaching when it would be invaluable, and when she would be unable to devote herself to these domestic duties.

The evenings were the most delightful, as has been stated. Then, the day's labour over and everything being in order, they would sit together in the little room at the back of the shop and chat, or read, or pursue some study or innocent amusement. Mr. Loveday fished out an old draught-board, with draughts and a set of chessmen, and was surprised to find that Nansie was by no means an indifferent draught-player, and that she knew the moves of chess, in which her skill was not so great. At one time of his life he had been fond of backgammon, and he taught Nansie the game, Timothy looking on and learning more quickly than the fair pupil whose presence brightened the home. Timothy also made himself proficient in the intricacies of chess, and within a few months justified himself master, and gave odds. An evening seldom passed without a reading from a favourite author, Nansie's sweet, sympathetic voice imparting a charm to passages from which something valuable might have been missed had they not been read aloud. From this brief description it will be gathered that Nansie's influence was all for good.

Thus time sped on, and Kingsley was still absent. He wrote to Nansie regularly, and she as regularly replied to his letters, never missing a post. She wrote in her bedroom always, and generally at night when •the others were abed. In silence and solitude she was better able to open her heart to her husband. To say that she was entirely happy apart from Kingsley would not be true, but she had a spirit of rare hope and contentment, and her gratitude for the shelter and comfort of her new home was a counterbalance to the unhappiness she would otherwise have experienced.

"A letter for you, Nansie," Mr. Loveday would say.

Taking it eagerly, she would speed to her room and read it again and again, drawing hopeful auguries from words in which none really lay. For although Kingsley's letters were cheerfully and lovingly written, there was nothing substantial in them in their prospects of the future. They were all of the present, of his doings, of his adventures, of his travels, of what he had seen and done, forming a kind of diary faithfully kept, but with a strange blindness in respect of years to come. At one time he was in France, at another in Italy, at another in Germany, at another in Russia.

"Mr. Seymour," he wrote, "has an insatiable thirst for travel, and will start off at an hour's notice from one country to another, moved seemingly by sudden impulses in which there appears to be an utter lack of system. It is inconvenient, but of course I am bound to accompany him; and there is, after all, in these unexpected transitions a charm to me who could never be accused of being methodical. The serious drawback is that I am parted from you. What pleasure it would give me to have you by my side! And you would be no less happy than I."

Then would follow a description of the places they passed through and stopped at, of people they met, and of small adventures which afforded him entertainment, ending always with protestations of love, the sincerity of which could not be doubted. But Mr. Loveday was never anything than grave when Nansie read aloud to him extracts from her husband's letters.

"Who is Mr. Seymour?" he asked.

"A gentleman," replied Nansie.

"What is he, I mean?" was Mr. Loveday's next question.

Nansie shook her head. "I have no idea."

"Has your husband any idea?"

"I suppose he has."

"You only suppose, Nansie."

"Yes, uncle, I can do nothing else, because Kingsley has never said anything about it."

"Surely, if he really knew," persisted Mr. Loveday, "he would not be so silent on the subject."

"Perhaps you are right, uncle; perhaps Kingsley does not really know."

"If Mr. Seymour were travelling with any specific object in view, there would be no need for secrecy. Say that he were an enthusiast, that he had a craze, no matter in what shape, he would not disguise it."

"Certainly not, uncle. Mr. Seymour must be travelling simply for pleasure."

"Which is not a simple matter, Nansie," observed Mr. Loveday, "when a man runs after it. I can imagine few things more laborious and less likely of a satisfactory result. Now, Nansie, what are your husband's duties in his employment?"

"He does not say, uncle."

"Do you think he has any?"

"I suppose so."

"More supposings, Nansie."

"What else can I say, uncle?"

"Nothing, my dear, and I am to blame for worrying you. We will drop the subject."

"No," said Nansie, earnestly, "please do not drop it."

"Why should we continue it, Nansie?"

"Because," replied Nansie, with a slight flush on her face, "I am afraid you are doing Kingsley an injustice."

"I should be sorry to do that," said Mr. Loveday, very seriously.

"I know you would," responded Nansie, in a tone of affection, "and that is why I want to set you right. You think that Kingsley is concealing something from me. He is not; he loves me too well. You think that I need some one to defend me. I do not. It is only when a person is wronged or oppressed that he needs a defender. No one has ever wronged or oppressed me. On the contrary, every one in the world is kind to me—that is," she added hastily in correction, for she thought of her husband's parents, "every one who knows me. Now you, uncle," she said, wistfully and tenderly, "before I came here I dare say you had no great regard for me."

"I had not, Nansie."

"It was only because you made a promise to my dear father out of your kind heart, and because you are an honourable man who would not break his word, that you welcomed me at first. And perhaps, too," her voice faltered a little here, "because I resemble my mother for whom you had an affection."

She paused, uncertain whether she had gone too far; but he inclined his head kindly towards her, and said:

"You are speaking justly, Nansie. Go on, if you have anything more to say."

"Yes, uncle, I have something more to say. That was your feeling for me at first; but since then—I say it humbly and gratefully—I have been happy in the belief that I have learnt something for myself."

"You have," said Mr. Loveday. "I love you, Nansie."

"It is so sweet to me to know it, dear uncle," said Nansie, with tears in her eyes, "that I am enabled to bear Kingsley's absence —I hope and pray it will not be for long— with courage and resignation. And because of that, because of the love which unites us, you must think well of Kingsley—you must think always well of him. Uncle, he is the soul of honour, truth, and unselfishness. When he told me he loved me, and asked me to marry him, he did not weigh the consequences, as nearly every other man in his position would have done."

"He was rash," observed Mr. Loveday.

"Would you censure him for it? Did

he not behave as an honourable, noble-hearted man?"

"Undoubtedly. He has a worthy champion in his wife."

"Ah, but it would distress me immeasurably to feel that you believe he needs a champion, or I a defender. You do not know him, uncle; when you do you will not fail to love him. I do not say that he is worldly wise, or quite fitted yet to battle with the future, but that it is his earnest desire to fit himself for what I feel will be a great struggle, and to perform his duty in a manly way. No man can do more, and, whatever may be our future, I shall love and honour him to the last."

"My dear Nansie," said Mr. Loveday, "say that you are partly right in your views of my feelings for your husband; be content now to know that you have won me over to his side."

"I am indeed content to know it, uncle."

"But should that deprive a man of his right to judge actions and circumstances? We sometimes condemn those whom we love best."

"It should not deprive him of the right," replied Nansie, adding, with what her husband would have told her was feminine logic, "but you must not condemn Kingsley."

"I will not. I will apply ordinary tests. When he took the situation with Mr. Seymour, did he know anything of his employer?"

"Nothing; but we were in great stress, and Kingsley was compelled to take advantage of his opportunity."

"Admitting that. But a man must face his responsibilities, and discharge them to the best of his ability."

"Yes, uncle, to the best of his ability."

"My dear, had you been a man, you would have made a very good special pleader. To continue. What is your husband's salary?"

A look of distress was in Nansie's eyes, and she did not reply.

"I infer," said Mr. Loveday, replying for her, "that you do not know."

"I fear I do," said Nansie, in a low tone.

"Tell me, then."

"I fear, uncle, that there is no salary attached to the situation."

"But there should be?"

"Yes, there should be."

"Mr. Seymour, wishing to engage a gentleman as part companion and part secretary, must have been prepared to enter into some kind of monetary arrangement. Whose fault is it that the arrangement was not made? I will reply for you again. It must have been Kingsley's fault. Not very practical, Nansie."

"I am afraid, uncle," said Nansie, speaking slowly, and as though she were about to commit an act of treason, "that Kingsley is not very practical."

"But how is a man to get along in the world," said Mr. Loveday, with a curious mixture of decision and helplessness, "who thus neglects his opportunities? I am speaking entirely in a spirit of kindness, Nansie."

"Yes, uncle, there's no occasion for you to remind me of that. But how can you blame Kingsley? He meets Mr. Seymour as one gentleman meets another. He is too delicate-minded to broach the subject of salary, and perhaps Mr. Seymour forgets it."

"No, child, Mr. Seymour does not forget it. He takes advantage of your husband, and the consequence is that he is using a man's services without paying for them. And the consequence, further, is that valuable time is being wasted and mis-spent. Two or three weeks ago you commenced to read to me something in one of your husband's letters, and you suddenly stopped and did not continue. It was about money. Am I wrong in supposing that what you were about to read was in reply to something you had written in a letter to your husband?"

"You are not wrong, uncle."

"Plainly, you asked him whether he could not send you a little money?"

"Yes."

"And that was his reply. I can judge what it was."

"Uncle, he had none to send. He is entirely dependent upon Mr. Seymour."

"Who is not liberal?"

"Yes, uncle."

"Who is not only not liberal, but unjust?"

"But that is not Kingsley's fault," pleaded Nansie.

"I am not so sure. Child, child, you and your husband are like the children in the wood, and you know their fate."

"I should be content," said Nansie, mournfully, for a moment overwhelmed—only for a moment; her mood changed instantly, and with indescribable tenderness she said: "But I want to live—to live!"

There was a new note in her voice, and in her eyes a dreamy look of exquisite happiness which caused Mr. Loveday to wonder as he gazed upon her. Never had she been so beautiful as she was at that moment. In the expression on her face was something sacred and holy, and Mr. Loveday saw that she was deeply stirred by emotions beyond his ken.

"Nansie!"

"Yes, uncle," said Nansie, awaking from her dream.

"You heard what I said?"

"Yes, uncle—but you must not blame Kingsley; you must not blame my dear husband."

"I will not—strongly. Only I should like you to consider what would have been your position if you had not found me in the London wilderness, or, having found me, if I had proved to be hard-hearted instead of a loving uncle."

"What is the use of my considering it," she asked, in a tone of tender playfulness, "when I did find you, and when you proved yourself to be the best of men? It would be waste of time, would it not? Confess now."

"Upon my word," said Mr. Loveday, "I should almost be justified in being cross with you if I did not suspect that any unreasonableness in our conversation must spring from me, in consequence of my not being familiar with the ways of women. But you shall not drive me completely from my point. For your sake, Nansie, I regret that I am poor. I never wished so much to be rich as I do at the present time. You are attending to me, Nansie?"

"Yes, uncle."

"Has your husband sent you any money at all since he has been away?"

"None, uncle. He has not had it to send."

"Yet you are in need of a little?"

She looked at him, and her lips trembled slightly; and then again, a moment afterwards, the same expression of dreamy happiness stole into her face which he had observed before.

"Yes, uncle, a little, a very little. But I shall manage; I have already earnt a trifle."

"In what way?" inquired Mr. Loveday, much mystified.

"I got some needlework to do and am being paid for it."

"But in the name of all that's reasonable," exclaimed Mr. Loveday, "where and when do you do your work?"

"In my room of a night, uncle," replied Nansie, blushing.

"When we are all asleep," said Mr. Loveday, with the nearest approach to a grumble she had heard from his lips. "This must not continue, Nansie. You will do your work here of an evening and during the day, if it is necessary."

"Yes, uncle, I will obey you. But——" her form swayed slightly, and she was compelled to make an effort to keep herself from swooning—"you must not be angry with me. I am not very strong just now."

She brought her work down, and went on with it before his eyes, and there was perfect harmony between them. But still, in the stillness of her room, when her uncle supposed her to be abed, her fingers were busy in their labour of tenderest love.

CHAPTER VI.

THE event which occurred in Mr. Loveday's house in Church Alley, and which caused him perhaps the greatest excitement in his life, will be explained by the following letter which Nansie wrote to her husband two months after the conversation between her and her uncle narrated in the last chapter.

"MY OWN DEAR KINGSLEY,

"At length I am strong enough to write to you, and it is a great joy to me to sit down once more to speak to the beloved wanderer of whom I think night and day. I am sure that you must be with me, in spirit, even in my dreamless sleep. You will not be sorry to know that you are not the only one now the thought of whom makes my heart a garden of flowers. I have a sweet treasure—surely the sweetest that ever blessed a happy woman—lying at my feet, and you will not begrudge me. Oh, my dear Kingsley, if you were with me at this moment, and we were looking down together on the lovely, innocent face of our darling, you would think as I do, that heaven itself was shining in the little room in which I am writing! Everything is so strangely beautiful that I can scarcely believe I am living the same life I lived till I became a happy, happy mother. It is not the same—it is sweeter, purer, more precious; I seem to hear angelic music even in the silence which surrounds me. I know what produces it. I put my face close to my darling's mouth, and I can just hear her soft breathing.

"You will forgive me, will you not, for

not having written to you for so long a time? I could not help it, you see. I know from your last letter that you received the one my uncle wrote to you, and that you would have flown to my side if you had had the means. It seems so cruel that you should be in such straits for money. Why do you not ask Mr. Seymour straightforwardly to pay you what he must owe you? It must be a good sum by this time. But perhaps it is wrong of me to say to you, why do you not do this or that?—for surely you must know what is best to be done, and the right time to do it. It is easy to judge for others, is it not, my dearest? I have the fullest faith and confidence in you; and, my dear, you must not worry about me. My uncle is the dearest friend I could have met with. He is kindness itself, and I feel that he loves me as if I were his daughter. And I have money—not much, Kingsley, dear, but enough —to go on with. Before baby came I earnt some, and presently, when she can crawl, and walk, and speak—oh, Kingsley, the wonder of it!—I shall earn more. Uncle is so good to me that I need very little; but still some things are necessary which uncle does not understand about, and he has not more than he knows what to do with. Then, of course, I am an expense to him; but he never makes the least mention of that—he is too considerate, and I know he is glad to have me with him—and to have baby, too, although I fancy he does not quite know yet what to make of the darling. Indeed, I half think he is frightened of her. I see him sometimes looking at her when she is asleep with such a funny look in his eyes that I can hardly keep from laughing. The idea of a great big man being frightened of a little baby! But, Kingsley, dear (I would not confess it to anybody but you), I, too, am frightened of baby a little sometimes, when she lies in my lap, staring at me solemnly with her beautiful eyes—the colour of yours, dearest—wide, wide open, without even so much as a blink in them. She seems to be reading me through and through. 'What are you thinking of, darling?' I whisper to her; and though of course she cannot answer me, I am sure that she understands, and that I should be very much astonished if I knew what was passing through her mind. She is going to be a very wise little body — I can see that—and very sweet and beautiful, and a great blessing to us. But she is that already, the greatest, the most precious that has ever fallen to my lot. You see, my dear husband, I look upon baby and you as almost one person; I cannot think of one without the other, it is impossible to separate you; so that when I say that baby is the greatest blessing that was ever given to me, I mean you as well as our darling. . . .

"I have been obliged to stop; baby

woke up, and we had a happy hour together. Now she is asleep again. She is so good, not at all fretful as some babies are, and when she cries (which is really not often) it is a good healthy cry, which makes uncle say that her lungs are in fine condition. . . .

"I have been reading over what I have written, and I stopped at the part where I speak of baby presently being able to walk and talk. Long before that, my dear Kingsley, I hope that you will be with us, and that we may be all living together. Do not think I am desirous of urging you to any other course than that which you consider right, but the happiness of our being together again would be so great! Is there any chance of Mr. Seymour coming to England and settling down here, and keeping you as his secretary at a fair salary? Then we could have a little home of our own, and you could go to Mr. Seymour in the morning and come home in the evening, and we should have one day in the week to ourselves. It is not a very great deal to ask for, but if some kind fairy would only grant it I should be supremely happy. Surely, surely, the future must have something good in store for us!

"I have told you in my letters all about Timothy Chance, and how good and helpful he has been. Well, my dear Kingsley, until baby came I looked upon Timothy as my knight, my own special cavalier whom I could depend upon for service at any hour I chose to call upon him; but I think now that he has divided his allegiance, at least half of it going to baby. Timothy is an extraordinary lad, and uncle has a great opinion of him. Putting his duties in uncle's business out of the question, and putting baby and me out of the question, Timothy seems to have only one idea—eggs and fowls. He is now the proud owner of four fine hens, and his spare minutes (not too many) are devoted to them. He reads up every book he can lay hands upon that treats of fowls, and is really very clever in his proceedings. He made me laugh by saying: 'If fowls won't lay they must be made to lay;' and he studies up food to coax them. It is very amusing; but Timothy is so earnest that you cannot help respecting him, and respecting him more because he is successful. He shows me his figures, and is really making a profit every month. He is now drawing out plans for constructing a movable fowl-house, in compartments, each compartment accommodating eight fowls, and capable of being taken down and put up again in a wonderfully short time. Uncle says the plans are as nearly perfect as possible, and that he should not wonder if Timothy made a fortune one of these fine days. Timothy has insisted upon my accepting two new-laid eggs a week. Uncle and he had some words about them at first, uncle wanting to pay for them and Timothy refusing to accept any money; but the good lad was so hurt and took it so much to heart that I persuaded uncle to let him have his way.

"Why do I write all this to you, dear Kingsley? To show you that I am in the midst of kindness, and that although you have not as yet been very fortunate, there is much to be grateful for. Remember our conversation, my darling, and never, never lose heart. Courage! courage! as you have said many times; and it will help you to feel assured that there are loving hearts beating here for you, and friends holding out willing hands. Why, if a poor, imperfectly educated lad like Timothy looks forward to making a fortune out of such simple things as eggs, what may you not do, with your advantages and education? All will be well, and there is a happy future before us.

"I am tired, and have a dozen things

to do, or I would keep on talking to you for hours. But I must really finish now. Baby sends you her dearest, dearest love. Indeed she does. I asked her, and upon my word, Kingsley, dear, she crowed and laughed. She is the most wonderful thing in the world, there is no doubt of that. I kiss her a hundred times for her dear papa, and I blow her kisses to you, and kiss them into the words I am writing. Our hearts are with you; our dearest love is yours. Oh, my darling! to close this letter is like bidding you good-bye again. Take all our love, which is for ever blossoming for you. I close my eyes, and think that you are by my side; and I press you to my heart, which beats only for you and our darling child. What name shall I give her?

"Good-bye, and God bless and guard you, my own dear love.

"Your faithful, loving wife,
"NANSIE."

CHAPTER VII.

HISTORY repeats itself. The fortunes of Timothy Chance were turned by a fire—whether for good or evil, so far as regards himself, had yet to be proved. He was to go through another experience of a similar kind, in which, as on the first occasion, those who befriended him were the greatest sufferers.

Nansie had to wait for more than a month before she received an answer to her last letter from Kingsley. He and his employer, it appears, had been continually on the move, and the letter which Mr. Loveday had written to him could not have reached him. It was by a lucky chance that Nansie's letter with the news that he was a father, fell into his hands after a long delay; and she gathered from his reply that some of his own communications to her must have miscarried. This last letter which she received was far from encouraging. It was in parts wild and incoherent; the cheerfulness which had pervaded his previous missives was missing; the writer seemed to be losing hope.

"I am learning some hard lessons," Kingsley wrote, "and am beginning to doubt whether there is any truth or justice left in the world."

This was distressingly vague, for no explanation of Kingsley's moody reflection was forthcoming. It did not even appear that he was drawing consolation, as he had often done during his absence, from the thought that Nansie was ever ready with open arms to comfort him.

"Instead of advancing myself," Kingsley wrote, "by the step I have taken, I have thrown myself back. It is a miserable confession to make, but there it is, and wherever I go I see, not the shadow, but the actual presentments of misery and injustice. Can any man inform me under what conditions of life happiness is to be found?"

As was to be expected, the letter was not wanting in affectionate endearments and in expressions of joy at the birth of their child. "He is miserable," thought Nansie, "because we are not together. When we are once more united, will it be wise to consent to another separation?" She felt that he had need for the companionship of a stronger nature than his own, and she prayed for the time to come quickly when she would be with him to keep his courage from fainting within him.

The very next day she was comforted by the receipt of another letter from Kingsley, in which was displayed his more cheerful, and perhaps more careless characteristics.

"What could I have been thinking of," he said, "when I wrote you such a strange, stupid letter as I did yesterday? I must have lost my wits, and I hasten to atone for it by sending you another in a better and more natural vein. Burn the first, my dear Nansie, so that it may not be in existence to reproach me. A nice piece of inconsistency you have married, my dear! I do not remember ever to have been so cast down as I have been for two or three days past; but I should keep that to myself, and not burden you with a share of my despondency. It has been my habit always to look with a light spirit upon circumstances, whether they were in my favour or against me; and if I am to replace that by becoming savage and morose, I shall be laying up for myself a fine stock of unhappiness. So I determine, for your sake and mine, and for the sake of your dear little bairn, to whistle dull care away, and to make the best of things instead of the worst. Here am I, then, my usual self again, loving you with all my heart and soul, longing to be with you, longing to hold our dear bairn in my arms, longing to work to some good end. The question is, how to set about it, and what kind of end I am to work for. There is the difficulty — to fall into one's groove, as we have decided when we have talked about things, and then to go sailing smoothly along. Yes, that is it, and we must set ourselves to work to find out the way. I may confess to you, my dear wife, that up to this point success has not crowned my efforts; in point of fact, to put it plainly, I am thus far a failure. However, I cannot see how I am to blame. If I had had the gift of prophecy I should never have joined Mr. Seymour, but how was one to tell what would occur? Now, my dear, you urge me to make some approaches to Mr. Seymour with respect to money matters. Well, awkward as the position is, I have endeavoured to do so, but have never got far enough, I am afraid, to make myself understood. My fault, I dare say, but just consider. There is nothing of the dependent in my relations with Mr. Seymour; he received me as an equal and we have associated as equals; when we first met there was no question raised as to a salary, and there has been none since. How, then, am I to go to him and say: 'You are indebted to me in such or such a sum'? It would be so coarse, and I do not see justification for it. If I have made a mistake I must suffer for it, and must not call upon another person to do so for me. That would not be consistent, or honourable, or gentlemanly. After all, my dearest, the standard of conduct is not arbitrary. What it would be right for Mr. Jones or Mr. Smith to do would not be right for me, and the reverse. What is to be done, then? Having made a mistake, I am too proud —perhaps not quite broken in yet— to get out of it in the most honourable way I can. It is in my power to say to Mr. Seymour: 'A thousand thanks for the pleasure you have afforded me and for the courtesies you have extended towards me, but my time is precious, and I must not keep away from my wife any longer.' That would be all right, but to follow it up with a request for a loan to enable me to get back to England would be so mean and coarse that I could never bring my tongue to utter the words. Can you understand my position, my darling? It is a humiliation to me to ask the question, but I am in a cleft stick, and am positively powerless to help myself. What a pity, what a pity that my original idea of living in a travelling caravan could not be carried out! Do you remember that delicious evening, dear? I should like to pass such another, and I dare say I should commit myself again to the foolish wish that it would last for ever.

"Now, my dearest, I am quite cheerful and light-hearted, but there is something I must tell you. I must warn you first, though, that this is a secret between ourselves; on no account must it be disclosed to your uncle or to any other person. Much may hang upon it—I do not know what; I prefer not to think; but at all events I must do nothing base or treacherous. If confidence has been reposed in me I must not betray it. But mark what I say, dear; it is only lately that I have come to a knowledge or a suspicion of certain things, and no hint must escape me of that knowledge or suspicion (it is a mixture of both) to any except yourself.

"In speaking of Mr. Seymour you would naturally suppose that you were speaking of an Englishman, the name being unmistakably English. But Mr. Seymour is not an Englishman, and therefore the name must be assumed. As to this I have no definite information, but it is so certainly. It did not occur to me to mention to you that Mr. Seymour was probably a foreigner, the matter seeming to be of such small importance. He speaks English fluently, with the slightest accent; speaks also French, German, Italian, and Russian, as to the precisely correct accent of any one of which I am not a competent judge. I am not given to curiosity, and have a habit of believing what I am told; that is, I do not look much below the surface of things. Now, this may lead a man into a scrape.

"Were I alone, without wife and child, I should, I dare say, allow myself to drift according to circumstances, but I am bound to consider you. Well, then, Mr. Seymour, with whose right name I am not acquainted, has ideas with which I am not sure whether I agree; he has a mission with which I am not sure whether I sympathise. There are large movements in public affairs which require deep investigation before one finally and firmly makes up one's mind. Take, for example, the revolutionary movement — the idea that all people should be upon an equality, the mission to bring this about. I had better not write to greater length upon this theme. If you do not quite understand my meaning I will explain it more fully when we are together again. In saying that I am deeply anxious to get back to England soon, and that I must by some means manage it, I am thinking more of you than of myself. Shortly before writing the letter which I sent to you yesterday, I allowed myself to be led away by certain disclosures which were made to me for the purpose of binding me to a certain course — Mr. Seymour and the friends he meets and makes thinking me ripe for it, perhaps, and giving me credit for being cleverer than I am; and it was an amateur enthusiasm which drove me to conclusions to which

I would prefer not to commit myself—again, more for you and our dear little one's sake than for my own. There! The confession is made; perhaps you can thread your way through my mysterious allusions. And now, my darling——"

Then the letter went on, and was concluded with expressions of love and tenderness, and occasional drifting into whimsical bypaths, in which the nature of the old Kingsley Nansie loved so well was faithfully depicted.

On that evening Nansie nerved her courage to speak to her uncle about Kingsley's desire to return to England, and her own that he should do so without delay.

"He is wasting his time," she said, "and cannot but feel it deeply that I am living upon your kindness."

"To which you are heartily welcome, Nansie," said Mr. Loveday.

"I know that, dear uncle; but is it as it should be?"

Without answering the question, Mr. Loveday said: "Certainly it would be better that your husband should be at some profitable work. It is a pity, Nansie, that you did not marry a man who was accustomed to work."

"It is not a pity, uncle. There is no better man in the world than Kingsley."

"It was only a reflection of mine, my dear," said Mr. Loveday. "There is no reason why Kingsley should not do well. But the getting back——"

"There is the difficulty, uncle," said Nansie, looking at him anxiously; "the getting back to London, and the commencement of a career."

"Well, my dear, we must do what we can. You would like to send him sufficient to bring him from foreign lands into our happy family circle. Understand, Nansie, that we are to live together. You have made me so accustomed to you that if you were to leave my house you would leave desolation behind you. I shall insist upon fair play. Unfortunately, funds are rather low just now, but I will manage it. Will ten pounds be enough?"

"I think it will, uncle. It must be as a loan, though we shall never be able to repay you for what you have done."

"There is nothing to repay, Nansie; you have given me more than value. Now we will shut up shop."

"So early?"

"Yes, if you want your husband back so quickly." He called Timothy, and gave him instructions to close. "I know where I can sell a parcel of books, and I must go and strike the bargain. I will take Timothy with me. While we are gone, write to your husband, and tell him that you will send him a draft for ten pounds to-morrow. Say, if you like, that you have borrowed it from me; it will make him feel more independent, and will show that he has a sincere friend in your old uncle. There, my dear! there is nothing to make a fuss over. A nice world this would be if we did not lend a helping hand to each other!"

While he was gone Nansie wrote her letter, and baby being asleep, ran out to post it. It was long since she had felt so happy and light-hearted. Kingsley was coming back; her beloved husband would soon be with them. Grave troubles had already entered into her life, but they seemed to vanish as she dropped her letter into the post-office box. All was bright again; Kingsley was coming back.

Returning, she related the good news to baby, and told her she must put on her best looks to welcome her papa. "And how happy we shall be, baby," she said, kissing the child again and again, "now and for evermore! You see, baby, papa is never going away again; never! never!"

The room in which she sat was the first

floor front, looking out upon Church Alley, and she saw a little ragged girl lingering outside. The girl looked hungry, and Nansie, with her baby in her arms, ran downstairs, and from the house, and gave the poor girl two-pence, which was all the money she had in her purse. The girl scudded away to the cook-shop, and Nansie went back to her room.

"There are so many," she said, addressing the baby again, "so many hundreds—ah! I am afraid, baby, so many thousands — worse off than we are; ever so much worse off, my darling pet. For they haven't got papa, have they? and they haven't got *you!* But the idea of my thinking that we are anything but well off, when we are going to be as happy as the days are long! I ought to be ashamed of myself, oughtn't I? You mustn't tell papa that I ever had a thought of repining, or it would grieve him. You must know, baby—I hope you are listening properly, sweet, with your great beautiful eyes so wide open, and looking so wise as you do—you must know, baby, that you have the very best and noblest papa that a baby ever had or ever could have. And he is coming home, and you must be very, very good, or you will frighten him away!"

Then she sang the child asleep, and sat in the dusk musing happily with her baby in her lap.

Suddenly she started to her feet with a look of alarm. She smelt fire. Snatching up her baby she ran into the rooms in which fires had been burning, but all was safe there, and she saw no cause for alarm. She was standing in the sitting-room looking about in her endeavour to account for the smell when a cry of "Fire!" from the adjoining house lent wings to her feet, and the next moment she was in the court, with a number of people about her in a state of great excitement. As to the cause of her alarm there was no doubt now. Tongues of flame darted from the windows, and instantaneously, as it seemed, slid into Mr. Loveday's shop. Hustled this way and that, and pressing her baby close to her breast, Nansie was so distracted that she could not afterwards give an intelligible account of what she saw; except that there appeared to be thousands of people thronging into Church Alley and being thrust back by the police, that the air was filled with flame and smoke and wild cries, that women were wringing their hands and screaming that they were ruined, that fire-engines were dashing up the narrow path, and firemen were climbing on to the roofs of the houses, and that, turning faint and reeling to the ground, she was caught by some humane person and borne to a safe house, where she and her baby received attention. She was unconscious of this kindness for some little while, and when she came to her senses Mr. Loveday and Timothy were bending over her. Timothy's face was quite white, and he was in a state of great agitation, but Mr. Loveday was composed and grave. The people in the room were saying it was a shame that the police would not allow him to go to his burning shop, but he, in answer, said that they were right in preventing him.

"What good could I do?" he said. "I should only be a hindrance. My great anxiety was for you, Nansie, and your baby, and when I heard you were here I came on at once. You must have received a terrible fright, my dear. You were not hurt, I hope?"

"No," she answered, she was not hurt, and she marvelled at his composure. Some other person in the throng was commenting audibly upon his calmness, and received for answer the reply from a neighbour that Mr. Loveday must be well insured.

"No," he said, turning to the speakers, "I am not insured for a penny."

They were surprised to hear this bad news, and poured condolence upon him.

"Uncle," whispered Nansie, pulling his head down to hers, "will it hurt you very much?"

"That has to be seen, my dear," he replied, with a cheerful smile.

"Not in spirits," she continued, gazing at him in pity and admiration; "I know now what real courage is. But in your business."

"If what I've heard is true," said Mr. Loveday, "I am being burnt out stock and block, and shall have no business left. In which case, Timothy, you will lose a situation."

"Don't think of me, sir," said Timothy, ruefully. "Think of yourself."

"I shall have plenty of time to do that, my lad."

"This is the second time," said Timothy, "that I've been burnt out of a situation. I had better not take another. I do nothing but bring misfortune upon my masters."

"Nonsense, Timothy, nonsense. It is the fortune of war, and we must fight through these defeats as best we can."

He asked for the mistress of the house they were in, and inquired whether she had a furnished room to let. There happened to be one fortunately on the second floor, and Mr. Loveday at once engaged it, and assisted Nansie upstairs. They had hardly been in the room a moment when the landlady appeared with a cradle for baby.

"It ain't mine," she observed; "Mrs. Smithson, next door, run and got it for you. She's a good creature is Mrs. Smithson, and has had seven of her own. She expects her next in about three weeks."

Nansie sent her thanks to Mrs. Smithson, and thanked the landlady also.

"Oh, that's all right," said the landlady. "Mothers are mothers, you know, and Mrs. Smithson is that fond of babies that it's my belief she could live on 'em." In which description of Mrs. Smithson's fondness for babies the landlady did not seem to consider that there was anything at all alarming. "And look here, my dear," she continued, "don't you take on. That's my advice—don't take on. The misfortune's bad enough, but there's worse, a thousand times. I'll see that you're nice and comfortable—and I say, Mr. Loveday, you can stop here a fortnight for nothing, you not being insured, and being always so kind and obliging to everybody. There's nobody better thought of than you, and it's a pity we ain't all of us rich."

"A great pity," said Mr. Loveday, shaking the landlady's hand, "and I am grateful to you for your offer; but I have no doubt we shall be able to scrape up the rent. If you could make my niece a cup of tea now."

"Ay, that I will," said the good woman, "and fresh, too, not the leavings; and she'll take it from me as a compliment, won't you, my dear?"

Nansie nodded with a cheerful smile, and the landlady, having leant over the baby and kissed it softly, and declared that it was the sweetest, prettiest picture that ever was, departed to make the tea.

"That is the best of misfortunes like this," observed Mr. Loveday; "it brings out the bright side of human nature. Sudden prosperity often has the opposite effect."

"But is it true, uncle," said Nansie, "that you will lose everything—everything?"

"There will in all probability be salvage," said Mr. Loveday, thoughtfully, "worth a pound or two, perhaps; maybe less. I shall prepare myself for the worst. Who is there?"

This was in response to a knock at the door, and Timothy presented himself with four new-laid eggs.

"We will accept them, my lad," said

Mr. Loveday. "How is the fire getting on?"

"They've got tight hold of it now, sir," replied Timothy, "and it's going down."

"And the shop, Timothy?" Timothy made no reply in words, but his face told the rueful tale. "Eh, well, it can't be helped. I'll be out presently and have a look round for myself. Yes," he continued when Timothy was gone, "I shall be prepared for the worst. Then all will be profit that falls short of my anticipations. I might worry myself by lamenting that I did not get insured, but it would do no good. Let me get it over by declaring that it was a piece of inconceivable folly to neglect so necessary a safeguard. The mischief is that I seldom if ever kept a balance in cash. As fast as it came in I spent it in fresh stock; it was a mania of mine, and I have paid for it. I shall have to commence the world over again, that is all. Nansie, my dear,

I regret what has occurred for your sake; it will, I fear, prevent my doing what I wished. We will not have anything hang over; it will be wisest to speak of what is in our minds. Did you write to your husband?"

"Yes, uncle."

"Is your letter posted?"

"Yes."

"Well, it cannot be recalled. If you will give me his address I will write to him before I go to bed, and make him acquainted with the calamity which has overtaken us. I think, Nansie, that I have learnt something of your character since you came to me, and I give you credit for possessing courage."

"I am not easily daunted, uncle. We are all of us learning lessons as we pass through life."

"They come in different shapes to different persons, and those are wise who can profit by experience. Some persons are overwhelmed by visitations of trouble; to some they impart new strength and vigour. Let this be the case with us; let us resolve not to be cast down, but to be up and doing with the best courage we can summon to our aid. It is a matter for thankfulness that bodily we are uninjured, and that baby is safe and well."

"You are a true comforter, dear uncle," said Nansie, pressing his hand.

"We might continue talking for hours, and could add little more to what we have already said and resolved. Here is our good friend, the landlady, with the tea. I will leave you together, and go and see how things are getting on."

"There are three houses gutted, they say," said the landlady, "yours and the one on each side of it. It is a mercy the whole alley isn't down."

"It is, and I am glad for those who have escaped."

"Don't go without a cup of tea, Mr. Loveday," said the landlady, "I've brought up one for you. I thought you would prefer it in your own room, my dear," she said, addressing Nansie, "there's such a lot of gossiping going on downstairs. Ah, that's sensible of you"—as Mr. Loveday took the cup of tea she poured out for him—"there's nothing like keeping up your strength. *You* must think of that, my dear, because of your baby. Half the neighbourhood wanted to come up and see you, but I wouldn't let 'em. If I put my foot down upon one thing more than another it's gossiping. They've found out how the fire occurred, Mr. Loveday."

"How was it?"

"It was that new lodger the Johnsons took in last week. He takes the room and keeps to it, and isn't known to do a stroke of work; he does nothing but drink. There was a lamp alight on the table, and some papers about. What does he do but upset the lamp, and then run away. He's drinking now at the 'Royal George.'"

"He was not hurt, then?"

"Not him! He had sense enough to run. Not that he could have done much good by stopping! But what I say is, he ought to be punished for it."

"So ought all confirmed drunkards. Fires are not the only mischief they cause. They break hearts and ruin useful lives. I will not be long, Nansie."

"What a man he is!" exclaimed the landlady, gazing after him admiringly. "There ain't another like him in all Whitechapel. Don't cry, my dear, don't cry; it won't be good for baby. With such a friend as your uncle, everything's sure to come right!"

CHAPTER VIII.

Mr. Manners, the great contractor, sitting in his study at a table spread with legal documents and papers relating to his vast transactions, was informed by a man-servant that a stranger wished to see him.

"Who is he?" inquired Mr. Manners.

"I don't know, sir."

"Did he not give you his name?"

"I asked him for it, sir, and he said you did not know him, but that he came on very particular business, and must see you."

"Must!"

"That is what he said, sir."

Mr. Manners considered a moment. He had finished the writing upon which he had been engaged, and had a few minutes' leisure.

"What kind of man?"

"Neither one kind nor another, sir."

"What do you mean?"

"That he might be a gentleman, sir, and mightn't. It's hard to say."

"It generally is nowadays. Show him in."

The servant retired, and ushering in Mr. Loveday, left the room.

"Well, sir?" said Mr. Manners. The contractor did not speak uncivilly, for the appearance of Mr. Loveday, who was fairly well attired, was in his favour; he might be a smaller contractor, or an inventor, or anything that was respectable.

"I have ventured to visit you, sir," said Mr. Loveday, "without first seeking an introduction, upon a matter of importance."

"My servant said upon particular business."

"He was scarcely correct, sir. I can

hardly call my errand business, but it is no less important than the most important business."

"It is usual to send in a card, or a name."

"My name you will probably recognise, and I did not give it to the servant from fear that you might have refused to see me."

"This sounds like an intrusion. What may be your name?"

"Loveday, sir."

Mr. Manners did not start or betray agitation, but he looked keenly at his visitor. He was a man of method, and had on all occasions complete control over his passions. He recognised the name, the moment it was uttered, as that of the girl for whom his son had deserted him. Therefore, the name of an enemy; undoubtedly the name of an intruder.

"It is a name with which you suppose me to be familiar?"

"Yes, sir."

"I ask the question simply because there are coincidences, and I make it a rule to avoid mistakes. If you come from my son——"

"I do not, sir."

"But you are in association with him? You know him?"

"Only indirectly, sir. I have never seen your son."

"I refuse to take part in mysteries. You are related to the young woman for whom my son threw over his duty to me."

"I am the young lady's uncle."

"And your visit is in furtherance of an appeal from her or on her behalf?"

"On her behalf, but not from her. I did not inform her that I was coming."

"The information is of no interest to me. The appeal you speak of is of the usual kind. It is superfluous to ask if you are rich."

"I am not, sir."

"Poor?"

"Yes, sir."

"Very poor?"

"Very poor."

His frankness, his bearing, his aspect compelled a certain amount of respect, and it did not soften Mr. Manners to be made to feel this.

"Had you any hand in this marriage?" demanded Mr. Manners.

"None, sir. Had my advice been solicited, I should have been strongly against it. I am not going too far to say that I should not have sanctioned it, and should have thrown in what small amount of authority I possessed to prevent it, if your consent had not been first asked and obtained."

This view of the matter appeared to strike Mr. Manners, and he regarded his visitor with closer attention; but presently he frowned; it was as though the honour of the alliance was on Nansie's side instead of Kingsley's.

"I will not inquire into your reasons," he said, "except in so far as to ask whether your brother, the young woman's father, who, I understand, is dead——"

"Yes, sir, he is dead."

"Whether he made any effort to prevent the marriage? I speak of it as a marriage, although I have my reasons for doubting whether it could have been legally entered into."

"Sir!" exclaimed Mr. Loveday, much astonished.

"I decline discussion," said Mr. Manners. "I am not an idle speaker, and I know what I mean. We will call it a marriage. It does not affect the conduct of my son towards me. You heard my question. If you have an objection to answer it I shall not complain."

"I have no objection, sir. My brother

knew nothing whatever of it until it was too late to interfere. The young people acted for themselves, without consulting a single person. It was a secret marriage."

Mr. Manners smiled. "Exactly. But my question is still not answered."

"My brother would have felt as I feel, sir. Without your sanction he would have withheld his consent, and would doubtless have succeeded in preventing the union."

"It would have been well if it had not taken place."

"I agree with you, sir."

Mr. Manners frowned again. His visitor was taking high ground.

"Come to the precise object of your visit," he said.

"The lamentable severance of the affectionate relations which existed between you and your son has been productive of much suffering. The young people have been driven hard—so hard that in the endeavour made by your son to obtain some sort of position which would hold out the hope of his being able to support her, they were compelled to separate. Your son went abroad and left his wife here in England, doubly orphaned, friendless, penniless, and unprotected. She appealed to me for shelter and temporary support, and I received her willingly, gladly. I will not indulge in sentiment, for I know you by repute to be a practical man, and it may be not only distasteful to you, but it may place me in a false light—as making a lame effort to influence you by means of which you may be suspicious; but it is due to my niece that I should declare in your presence that a sweeter, purer, more lovable woman does not breathe the breath of life. She is a lady, well educated, gentle, and refined; and whatever value you may place upon my statement — which I solemnly avow to be true—you must agree that it is to the credit of your son that if he chose for his mate a lady who was poor, he at least chose one who, if fortune placed her in a high position, would be fitted to occupy it. Of this it is in your power to assure yourself, and you would then be able to judge whether I speak falsely or truly. Your son has been absent from England now for many months, and from his letters to his wife it may be gathered that he has been disappointed in his hopes and expectations, and it is certain that he has not benefited pecuniarily by the effort he made."

"He is reaping the fruits of his disobedience," said Mr. Manners.

Mr. Loveday made no comment on the interruption, but proceeded. "The consequence is that he has been unable to send his wife the smallest remittance. Until to-day this has been of no importance, as I was in a position to discharge the obligation I took upon myself when I received her into my home. Your son's affairs abroad became so desperate (and, in one vague sense, possibly compromising) that it was decided yesterday between my niece and myself to send him money to bring him home, in order that he might make another effort here to obtain a livelihood. I am speaking quite plainly, sir, and without ornament of any kind, and you will see to what straits your son is reduced."

"He is justly served," said Mr. Manners.

"It was but a small sum of money that was required," continued Mr. Loveday, "but I did not possess it. I had, however, books which I could sell—I am a bookseller by trade, sir—and last evening I left my house and place of business to negotiate the sale. Meanwhile my niece wrote to your son that I would supply her with the means for his return home, and that she would send him the money to-day. Upon my return, two or three hours later, I found my house in flames. The account of the fire, with my name, is in this morning's papers, and you may verify my statement. I was not insured, and nothing was saved. I am a beggar."

"It is, after all, then," said Mr. Manners, with a certain air of triumph, "on your own behalf that you are making this appeal to me."

"No, sir," replied Mr. Loveday, "I want nothing for myself; I shall rub along somehow, and hope to lift my head once more above adverse circumstance. My appeal is on behalf of your son's wife. I am unable to fulfil the promise I made to furnish her with the small sum required to bring your son home. I ask you respectfully and humbly to give it to me or to send it to her direct to this address." He laid a piece of paper, with writing on it, on the table. "If you would prefer to hand it to her personally she will call upon you for the purpose."

"You have spoken temperately," said Mr. Manners, with cold malice in his tones. "What is the amount you require?"

"Ten pounds, sir," replied Mr. Loveday, animated by a sudden and unexpected hope.

Mr. Manners touched a bell on his table. A servant appeared.

"Show this person to the door," he said.

"Is that your answer, sir?" asked Mr. Loveday, sadly.

"Show this person to the door," repeated Mr. Manners to the servant.

"I implore you," said Mr. Loveday, strongly agitated. "When I tell you that you have a grandchild but a few weeks old; that the poor lady, your son's wife, is in a delicate state of health——"

"Did you hear what I ordered?" said Mr. Manners to the servant, and repeated again: "Show this person to the door."

CHAPTER IX.

From that day commenced for Nausie and her uncle the hard and bitter battle of life. All that had gone before was light in comparison. Without money, without friends in a position to give them practical assistance, they had to depend upon themselves for the barest necessities. Confident and hopeful as he was, Mr. Loveday found it impossible to raise a new business out of the ashes of the fire which had ruined him.

"I must begin again," he said.

Had any employment offered he would have accepted it, however uncongenial it might have been; but nothing came his way. Golden apples only fall to those who have already won fortune's favours. To those most in need of them they are but visions.

He was not the kind of man to waste his time; besides, he knew how precious it was. An idle day now would be inviting even harder punishment in the future. As the mountain would not come to Mahomet, Mahomet went to the mountain—that is, to a newspaper office, where he laid out a shilling or two in fourth and fifth editions, and bravely hawked his wares in the most likely thoroughfares. The day's labour over, he found himself the richer by nineteen pence.

"Come now," he said to Nansie, gaily, "that is not so bad. In a little while we shall grow rich."

His thought was, not that nineteen pence a day would make them rich, but would keep the wolf from the door. Strange that in this the most civilised of countries we should snatch a phrase pregnant with terror from savage times and savage lands.

"The great difficulty," he said, "is my voice. Young rascals beat me with their lungs. They ring out the news; I can but quaver out the tempting morsels of murders and suicides. How I envy the youngsters! Still I shall manage, I shall manage."

Both he and Nansie had secret thoughts which they kept from each other.

"Three mouths to feed," thought Nansie. "It would be easier for him had he but his own."

"She must not think she is a burden to me," thought Mr. Loveday, "or I shall lose her."

He would have suffered anything to prevent a separation. Strong human links grew out of her helplessness; he was Nansie's protector, and it made him glad. In those early days of the new struggle she could do nothing to help the home, which consisted of two very small rooms at the top of a working man's house. The fright of the fire had weakened her, and weeks passed before she was strong enough to put her shoulder to the wheel. Her uncle did not tell her of his visit to Kingsley's father; silence was the truest mercy. And it happened that within a very short time doubts of Kingsley's faithfulness and honesty rose in his mind. The cause of this lay in the fact that from the day of the fire no letter from Kingsley reached them. It made him indignant to note Nansie's sufferings as day after day passed by without news.

"Do you think the letters have miscarried?" she asked.

"Letters don't miscarry," replied Mr. Loveday.

She looked at him apprehensively; his voice, if not his words, conveyed an accusation against the absent one.

"You believe he has not written," she said.

"I am sure he has not written," said Mr. Loveday.

"Then something must have happened to him," she cried. "He is ill and penniless, and I cannot help him!"

"If I had but a magic ring," thought Mr. Loveday, but he said no word aloud.

He reasoned the matter out with himself. On one side an innocent, unworldly, trustful woman of the people; on the other, the son of a man of fabulous wealth awakened from his dream. For this summer-lover, here was a life of poverty and struggle; there, a life of luxury and ease. To judge by human laws, or rather, by the laws which governed the class to which Kingsley Manners belonged, which path would the young man choose? "It is more than likely," thought Mr. Loveday, "that the scoundrel has made his peace with his father, and has resolved to

cast her off. But he is her husband"——
His contemplations were suddenly arrested. Words uttered by Kingsley's father recurred to him. "I speak of it as a marriage, although I have my reasons for doubting whether it could have been legally entered into." What if there was some foundation for these words? What if they were true? He did not dare to speak to Nansie of this. She would have regarded it as base and disloyal, and the almost certain result would have been to part them for ever. So he held his peace out of fear for himself, out of pity for her.

Thus three months passed. Nansie had regained her physical strength, but her heart was charged with woe.

"I cannot bear this suspense any longer," she said to her uncle. "I will go to Kingsley's father, and ask him if he has received any news of my husband."

Mr. Loveday did not attempt to dissuade

her; he thought that good might come of the visit, if only in the opening of Nansie's eyes to Kingsley's perfidy, of which by this time he was fully convinced. He did not offer to accompany her, knowing that it would lessen the chances of Mr. Manners' seeing her.

She went early in the morning, and sent up her name to the great contractor, and received his reply that he would not receive her. She lingered a moment or two, and cast an imploring glance at the man-servant as though it were in his power to reverse the fiat, but the man looked impassively first at her, then at the door, and she left the house.

What a grand, stately house it was! It almost made her giddy to look to the top. She stood on the other side of the road, watching the door through which she had just passed; her mind was made up to wait, and at all risks to accost Mr. Manners when he came out. She had never seen him, but she was sure she would know him when he appeared. Kingsley had shown her the portrait of his father, and the likeness between them would render mistake impossible. She wondered whether it would have assisted her to bring her baby girl, and wondered, too, how a man so rich and powerful as Mr. Manners could have the heart to behave so harshly to his only child. She had gone no farther than the entrance hall of the stately mansion, but the evidences of wealth which met her eyes had impressed her more deeply than ever with the sacrifice Kingsley had made for her sake. A sense of wrong-doing came to her. She should not have accepted the sacrifice. She should have thought of the future, and should not have allowed herself to be led away by the impetuous passion of her lover. Even the duty she owed to her dear father had been neglected, and she had taken the most solemn step in life without consulting him. It was too late to turn back now, but could she not atone for the wrong she had done? If she said to Kingsley: "Dear husband, let us part; return to your father's home, to your father's heart, and I will never trouble you more;" would he accept the atonement? Would he, would he? A chill fell upon her heart, like the touch of an icy hand, but the sweet remembrances of the past, of the vows they had exchanged, of the undying love they had pledged to each other, brought gleams of sunshine to her. Kingsley had thrown in his lot with her for weal and woe. She would work, she would slave for him, and he should never hear one word of complaining from her lips. If only they were together again! They could be happy on a very little; she would make him happy; she would be bright and cheerful always, and he would draw gladness from her. Their baby was at home, waiting for a father's kisses, for a father's love. If he needed a stronger incentive to be true and faithful, he would find it in his child. Upon the mere suggestion of this possibility she stood up in defence of him. No stronger incentive was needed than the ties which already bound them together. But where was he? What was the reason of his long and heart-breaking silence?

She walked slowly up and down for an hour and more, never losing sight of the door of the rich man's house. She was determined not to go away without seeing him, if she had to remain the whole of the day. It was a weary, anxious time, and it was fortunate for her that she had not much longer to wait. The door opened, and Mr. Manners came forth.

How like he was to Kingsley!—only that his face was harder, and that all that was gentle and tender in Kingsley's face was depicted in his father's in hard, stern lines.

But the likeness was unmistakable. He stopped as she glided swiftly to his side and timidly touched his sleeve.

"Well?"

His voice was as hard and stern as his face, and if she had not nerved herself to her task the opportunity would have been lost.

"You would not see me when I called at your house, sir, and I took the liberty of waiting for you here."

He did not ask who she was, and he showed no sign that he was touched by her gentle, pleading manner.

"What do you want?"

"I came, sir, to ask if you had any news of"—she stopped short at the name of Kingsley; he might have resented it as a familiarity—"of your son."

"Why come to me?"

"I do not know, sir," said Nansie, humbly, "whether I dreaded or hoped that you might relieve me of the trouble which is oppressing me; but you may have heard from him lately."

"I have not heard from him."

"Do you know nothing of him, sir?"

"Nothing; nor do I wish to know. When he left my house he was aware that the step he took put an end to all relations between us. I am not a man to be turned from my purpose. He chose his course deliberately, and set me at defiance."

"No, sir, no!" cried Nansie. "He had no thought of that."

"Words do not alter facts. He owed me a plain duty, and he ignored it for a stranger. The lures you used to entangle and ruin him have proved effectual. You led him on to his destruction, and you are reaping what you have sown. Finish your errand."

"It is finished, sir," said Nansie, turning mournfully away. "I cannot doubt that you have spoken truly, and that you have not heard from my husband. The last time he wrote to me he was in sore distress, without means to return home. I was in hopes that I should be able to send him a little money, but my hope was destroyed by a calamity which beggared the only friend I have."

"I have heard something in the same strain. You sent this only friend to me."

"No, sir, I did not. Do you mean my uncle?"

"I mean him. He came to me, as you know, and asked me for a sum of money to send abroad to my son."

"Indeed, indeed, sir, I did not know it."

"Which, doubtless," continued Mr. Manners, ignoring the contradiction, "he would have pocketed, with the satisfactory thought that he had got something out of me."

"You do my uncle great injustice, sir. He is noble and generous, and I honour him with my whole heart."

"Yes, yes," said Mr. Manners, and there was a deeper sternness in his voice, "it is among the class to which you and he belong, and into which you have dragged my son, that honour and nobility are to be found. I have had experience of it. Once more, finish your errand."

"I have nothing more to say, sir. I fear to anger you."

"Your real purpose in seeking me was to beg for money."

"Indeed not, sir. I had no such purpose."

"And would not accept it if I offered it?"

"I cannot with truth say that, sir. We are so poor that the pride I once had is broken. Pardon me if I say that I think you have no intention of offering it."

"I have none."

She bowed, and crossed to the opposite side of the road; but before she had gone a dozen yards she heard his voice, accosting her.

"It is in my mind to say something to you."

She turned to him with a sudden hope. Had he relented? Had her distress softened his heart towards her? A glance at his face dispelled the hope. There was in it no sign of pity.

"Accompany me to my house," he said.

Bewildered and surprised she walked by his side in silence, and they entered the mansion together.

"You would probably like," said Mr. Manners, "to have some better knowledge than you at present possess of the position which, by his disobedience and unfilial conduct, my son has forfeited."

CHAPTER X.

HE conducted her through some of the principal apartments, which had been furnished and decorated in a princely style. The pictures, the sculptures, the bric-à-brac were of the choicest character. Her feet sank in the thick, soft carpets, and her heart fainted within her as she followed Mr. Manners through the sumptuously appointed rooms. He paused before one, and throwing open the door:

"You may enter: it was my son's bedroom."

She obeyed him, a rush of tears almost blinding her; Mr. Manners remained outside. She saw, not a bedroom, but a suite of rooms luxuriously furnished; a library of costly books; rare old engravings on the walls; a bath-room fitted up with all the newest appliances; everything that money could purchase to make a man's life pleasant and devoid of care. She remained there but a short time; the contrast between these rooms and the miserable attics which she and her uncle occupied, and to which she hoped to welcome Kingsley, appalled her. When she rejoined Mr. Manners in the passage, he led her downstairs, and ushered her into his study.

"You may sit down," he said.

She was tired, wretched, and dispirited, and she accepted the ungracious invitation.

"I am not in the habit of boasting of my wealth," he said; "what you have seen affords proof of it. And all that you have seen, with means sufficient to keep it up ten times over, would have been my son's had you not marred his career. I will not do you an injustice; you have surprised me; I thought that my son had taken up with a common, vulgar woman; I find myself mistaken."

Again animated by hope, she looked up; again her hope was destroyed by the stern face she gazed upon.

"It is because I see that you are superior to what I anticipated that I am speaking to you now. Doubtless my son has informed you that by my own unaided exertions I have raised myself to what I am." She bowed her head. "The pleasure of success was great, and was precious to me, not so much for wealth itself, but for a future I had mapped out, in which my son was to play the principal part. With him absent, with him parted from me, this future vanishes, and I am left with the dead fruits of a life of successful labour. Who is to blame for this?"

She held up her hands appealingly, but he took no notice of the action.

"You are therefore my enemy, and not only my enemy, but my son's. With my assistance, with my wealth and position to help him, he would have risen to be a power in the land. You have destroyed a great future; you have deprived him of fame and distinction; but there is a remedy, and it is to propose this remedy to you that I invited you into my house. Your speech is that of an educated person, and you must be well able to judge between right and wrong. What your real character is I may learn before we part to-day. I will assume, for instance, that you are nothing but an adventuress, a schemer — do not interrupt me; the illustration is necessary to what I have to say. You may be nothing of the kind, but I assume the possibility to give force to a statement I shall make without any chance of a misunderstanding. It is this. Assuming that you played upon my son's feelings because of my being a rich man, in the expectation that if not at once, in a little while I should open my purse to you, it will be well for you to know that there is not the remotest possibility of such an expectation being realised. Do you understand?"

She did not reply in words; the fear that she might further anger him kept her silent; she made a motion which he interpreted into assent, and accepting it so, continued:

"Assuming, on the other hand, that you did not weigh the consequences of your conduct, and that you had some sort of a liking for my son——"

"I truly loved him, sir," she could not refrain from saying.

"It shall be put to the proof. If you love him truly you will be willing to make a sacrifice for him."

"To make him happy," she said, in a low tone, "to bring about a reconciliation between you, I would sacrifice my life."

"But it is not yours to sacrifice. Something less will do. On one condition, and on one condition only, will I receive and forgive my son."

And then he paused; it was not that the anguish expressed in her face turned him from his purpose, but that he wished her to be quite calm to consider his proposition.

"I am listening, sir."

"The condition is that you shall take a step which shall separate you from my son for ever."

"What step, sir?"

"There are other lands, far away, in which under another name, you can live with your uncle. You shall have ample means; you shall have wealth secured to you as long as you observe the conditions; you shall not be interfered with in any way; you will be able to live a life of ease and comfort——"

He did not proceed. There was that in her face which arrested his flow of language.

"Is Kingsley to be consulted in this, sir?"

"To be consulted? Certainly not. He is not to know it."

"Shall I be at liberty to write and tell him that it is for his good I am leaving him?"

"You will not be at liberty to communicate with him in any way, directly or indirectly."

"He is, then, to suppose that I have deserted him?"

"He is to suppose what he pleases. That will not be your affair."

Indignation gave Nansie courage. "Is it to be yours, sir?"

"What do you mean?" demanded Mr. Manners, frowning.

"That you will have the power to invent some story to my discredit, and that your son shall be made to believe I am not worthy of him. That is my meaning, sir."

"Do you think you are serving him or yourself by the tone you are adopting?" asked Mr. Manners, rising from his chair.

It was an indication to Nansie, and she obeyed it and stood before him.

"I have not thought of that, sir; I am thinking only of what is right. Forgive me for having intruded myself upon you, and allow me to leave you. If your son is living—sometimes in my despair I fear the worst, he has been so long silent—and returns home, perhaps you will inform him of the proposition you have made to me and of the manner in which I received it."

"That is a threat that you will do so."

"No, sir, it is not; he will hear nothing from me. Heaven forbid that by any future act of mine I should help to widen the breach between you! Good morning, sir."

She did not make her uncle acquainted with what had passed between Mr. Manners and herself; she simply said that Mr. Manners had refused to see her, that she had waited for him in the street, and that she had learnt from him that he had not heard from Kingsley.

"Did he speak kindly to you?" asked Mr. Loveday.

"No; he is bitterly incensed against me, and looks upon me with aversion. If I had ever a hope that he would relent towards us, it is gone now for ever. Uncle, is it my fancy that you are looking strangely at me?"

"Your fancy, my dear," replied Mr. Loveday, with a smile which he endeavoured to make cheerful. "Why should I look strangely at you? Your interview with Mr. Manners has unnerved you."

"Yes," said Nansie, "it must be so. When Kingsley returns he must not know of my visit to his father. It will make him angry and uncomfortable."

"I shall not tell him, my dear," said Mr. Loveday.

CHAPTER XI.

When Kingsley returns! Nansie suppressed a sigh as she uttered the words; but the unspoken thought was in her mind: " Would he ever return?" She flew to her baby as to a refuge and a sanctuary, but her heart was very heavy.

It was not her fancy that her uncle had looked strangely at her, and he had not behaved ingenuously in his reply to her question. He had deep cause for uneasiness, and his duty seemed to lie, for the present, in the effort to keep her in ignorance of ominous news which had come to his knowledge during her visit to Kingsley's father.

On the previous day, in the last edition of the papers he sold in the streets he noticed a paragraph to which he had paid no particular attention. It was simply the record of an accident on a German railway, in which ten persons had been killed and considerably more than that number seriously hurt. No particulars were given, and no names were mentioned. In the first edition of this day's evening papers Mr. Loveday read the following:

"Further particulars have reached us of the railway accident in Germany, but its precise cause still remains unexplained. It appears that the train was conveying nearly two hundred travellers, of whom ten met their death, as was stated yesterday, and twenty-three were seriously injured. Among the dead was a gentleman of the name of Seymour, who was accompanied by Mr. Manners, who is supposed to have been travelling with Mr. Seymour as a kind of companion or secretary. These two are the only English names in the list given of killed and wounded. Mr. Manners is one of those who were seriously injured; he lies now in a precarious state which precludes the possibility of any information being obtained from him which would enable the authorities to communicate with his relatives or the relatives of Mr. Seymour. As to the latter, however, some important discoveries have already been made through documents found upon his person. Reticence has been observed in making these particulars public, but sufficient is known to warrant the statement that, despite the English name under which he travelled, he is by nationality a Russian and that he occupied a position of responsibility in a certain secret revolutionary society whose aim it is to spread discontent and disaffection among the working classes on the Continent."

It was this paragraph which caused Mr.

Loveday so much anxiety. There could be no mistake that the Mr. Manners referred to was Nansie's husband; the association of his name with that of Mr. Seymour rendered this a certainty, and it appeared to Mr. Loveday that the personal injuries he had met with in the railway accident were not the only dangers which threatened him. Mr. Loveday could not immediately make up his mind whether it would be wise to acquaint Nansie with what had come to his knowledge. It was very unlikely that she would otherwise hear of it, for the reason that she never read the newspapers; in the neighbourhood in which they lived an accident so remote would pass unnoticed, and thus it would not be difficult to keep her in ignorance of her husband's peril. Kingsley's father could not have known anything of this when he and Nansie were together, or he would undoubtedly have made some reference to it.

What was best to be done? That was the question which was perplexing Mr. Loveday. To take any practical step was out of his power, because that would entail the expenditure of money which he did not possess. He and Nansie were living now literally from hand to mouth; the day's earnings sufficed for bare daily food; they had not a shilling to spare from the inexorable necessities of existence. To make another appeal to Mr. Manners would be worse than useless; it would bring fresh insults and revilings upon them from the stern millionaire whose heart was steeled against the calls of common humanity. Thus did he argue with himself as to the good that would be done by making the disclosure to Nansie; it would but intensify the sorrow caused by Kingsley's silence into a torture which would be unendurable. If any useful end could have been served by letting Nansie into the secret of her husband's peril, Mr. Loveday would not have hesitated to inform her of it; but, so far as he could see, the distress of mind occasioned by the revelation would add misery to misery; and after some long consideration of the matter he determined to keep the matter to himself, at least for the present. Meanwhile he watched the papers for further information of the railway accident, but for some time saw no reference to it. One day, however, the following paragraph arrested his attention :

"With respect to Mr. Seymour who met his death in the railway accident in Germany, the particulars of which have been fully reported in our columns, it is now certain that he was by birth a Russian, and that he was for a number of years intimately connected with conspiracies against law and order. The documents found upon his person were of such a character, and were so drawn out, as to destroy the hope that was entertained that they would lead to the detection of the members of the secret societies with which he was associated. Great pains have evidently been taken—probably from day to day — to do away with all documentary evidence that would incriminate others, and this is an indirect proof of the dangerous nature of the conspiracies in which he was engaged. With respect to the Mr. Manners who met with serious injuries, nothing to directly implicate him has come to light. The strongest point against him is the fact of his having travelled for many months with Mr. Seymour on apparently confidential relations. Papers found in his possession lead to the conclusion that he is the son of the great contractor, Mr. Valentine Manners, whose name is known all the world over."

In the following day's paper Mr. Loveday read a letter to the following effect:

" SIR,—It is necessary for me to state that

I have not been in any way acquainted with the late movements and proceedings of my son, Mr. Kingsley Manners, who is reported to have met with serious injuries in a railway accident in Germany, nor have I any knowledge of the Mr. Seymour with whom he is said to have travelled as companion.

"Faithfully yours,

"Valentine Manners."

That was all. Although Mr. Loveday carefully searched the papers day after day, he saw no further reference to the matter; it dropped out of sight, as it were, and the faint interest it had excited in the public mind appeared to have died completely away. The hard battle of life continued sadly and monotonously, without the occurrence of one cheering incident to lighten the days; and as time wore on Nansie ceased to speak to her uncle of the beloved husband who was either dead or had forgotten her. In her sad musings upon the question of death or forgetfulness, she did not bring the matter to an issue. Had she been compelled to do so, she would have stabbed herself with the torture that Kingsley was dead; for that he could have forgotten her, and that he could be systematically neglecting her, was in her faithful, chivalrous heart impossible. All that she could do was to wait, although hope was almost dead within her.

At an unexpected moment, however, the question was solved.

It was evening. Mr. Loveday had not returned from his daily labours, and Nansie had put her baby asleep in her cradle, and had gone out to execute some small household duties. She hurried through them as quickly as possible, and, returning home, had almost reached the street door of the house in which she lived, when a voice at her back said:

"It *is* Nansie!"

The pulses of her heart seemed to stop. It was her husband's voice, and so overcome was she by this sudden ray of sunshine that, when she turned, she could scarcely see before her. Again the voice came to her ears; the gay, light, happy voice of old, which expressed only joy and sweetness, and in which there was no note of sadness or sorrow.

"Why, Nansie—it *is* Nansie! I was born under a lucky star."

And still, without seeing the speaker, she felt herself drawn to the heart of the one man in the world she loved — of the dear husband and the father of the babe sleeping peacefully at home.

"Oh, Kingsley! Is it you, is it you?"

"Of course it is, Nansie. Who else should it be? But it is very perplexing and puzzling; I don't quite see my way out of it. Tell me, Nansie—you expected me, did you not?"

"Yes, Kingsley, yes—for so long, for so long!"

"No, no, not for so long. Why, it can have been but a few days since I went away! Let me see—how was it? We had to look things in the face, and we did, and we agreed that something must be done, and then—and then—upon my word, Nansie, I think I am growing worse than ever; I not only fly off at a tangent, but I seem to be afflicted by an imp of forgetfulness. What does it matter, though? I have found you, and we are together again."

During this speech, Nansie's eyes were fixed upon his face in tender love and thoughtfulness. His words were so at variance with the true nature of her position and his, that she would have been unable to understand them if love had not brought wisdom to her. There was in Kingsley's eyes the same whimsical expression as of old, there was in his manner the same light-heartedness which had enabled him to look upon the future without anxiety, the tones of his voice were clear and gay, but he bore about him an unmistakable air of poverty. His clothes were worn threadbare, his hands were attenuated and almost transparent, and the lines of his face denoted that he had passed through some great suffering. He evinced no personal consciousness of these signs, and seemed to be at peace and in harmony with himself and all around him.

"Are you well, Kingsley?" asked Nansie, solicitously.

"Well, my love? Never was better in my life, and now that I have found you, there is nothing more to wish for. And yet—and yet——"

He passed his hand across his forehead, and looked at her in a kind of humorous doubt.

"Do you observe anything singular in me, my love?"

It would have been cruel to have answered him with the direct truth. It was from the deep well of pity with which her heart was filled that she drew forth the words:

"No, Kingsley, no."

"Are you sure?"

"Yes, dear."

"I am glad to hear you say so, Nansie. I am the same as ever, eh?"

"Yes, Kingsley, the same as ever; but we will not part again."

"No, indeed! I don't intend that we shall—because, although we have been separated but a short time, my head has got full of fancies about this and that—foreign countries—outlandish places—strange people—rapid journeys—accidents even, but dreams, all of them, Nansie. They must be dreams, or I could fix them with greater certainty. Now, you know my old way, my dear; when anything was troubling me I used to say: 'What is the use? It won't make things better.' There is only one wise way to look upon life—make light of things. You remember a favourite saying of mine—it was from a song, I think, was it not? 'Never trouble trouble, till trouble troubles you.' And that is the way we will go through life together, eh, my love?"

"Yes, Kingsley," said Nansie, and would have said more, but for a sudden trembling that came over him, which caused him to cling to her for support.

"What is the matter, Kingsley?"

"To tell you the truth, my dear," he replied, with a wan, whimsical smile, "you would hardly believe it, but I think I am hungry!"

"Hungry! Oh, Kingsley!"

"Well, yes; such a careless, neglectful fellow as you have got for a husband, Nansie, never thinking of things at the right moment, never taking into account that it is necessary to eat even, until it is forced upon him that he must eat to live. And talking of eating to live—is there anything in the larder, Nansie?"

He had rallied a little, and spoke with greater firmness.

"Yes, Kingsley, plenty; come — come. Ah, my dear, my dear, with all my heart I thank God that you are with me again!"

"Dear wife," he murmured, and allowed himself to be led by her into the house, and up the dark stairs to the rooms she occupied.

But outside the door, on the landing, she whispered to him:

"Kingsley!"

"Yes, love."

"There is a great happiness within. Be prepared for it."

"There is a great happiness here"—with his arms around her. "I am really and truly thankful."

"But a greater within, Kingsley, my husband. Listen—our darling child sleeps there."

"Our darling child, our little one! Surely

I have seen her in my dreams, in which I have seen so many strange things. Ah, how I have dreamt of you, Nansie, even during this short absence! But let us go in, or I shall be reproached for forgetfulness."

They entered the room together, they leaned over the cradle, they knelt by its side, and Kingsley, lowering his face to the pretty babe sleeping there, kissed her softly and tenderly.

"She is very sweet, Nansie, like you. I am sure her eyes are the colour of yours."

"No, darling, she has your eyes."

"And your heart, Nansie. Happy little one, happy little one! We will make her happy, will we not, dear?"

"Yes, Kingsley."

"But, my dear, pardon me for saying so, I am really and truly hungry. Even a piece of dry bread would be acceptable."

She kept back her tears, and quickly placed bread upon the table, which he ate ravenously at first, smiling at her gratefully the while. Very soon she had prepared some hot tea, which he drank, and begged her to drink a cup with him. His hunger being appeased, he lay back in his chair, his eyes wandering round the room.

"What is our dear little one's name?" he asked; "I have forgotten it."

"No, dear," said Nansie, "you have not forgotten it, because she has not one yet; we call her 'baby,' you know."

"Yes, yes," he said, "'baby,' of course, the best, the sweetest that ever drew breath; but she must have a name, Nansie; she cannot go through life as 'baby.' Say that when she is a happy woman she marries, it would not do for her to be called 'baby' then."

"We waited for you, Kingsley, to give her a name."

"Well, then, what shall it be? But that it would introduce confusion into our little home, no better name than 'Nansie' could be found. That would not do, would it?"

"No, Kingsley. Shall we give her your mother's name?"

"My mother's? No, there must be none but good omens around her. *Your* mother's, Nansie. I remember you told me it was Hester."

Then he called aloud, but in a gentle voice, "Hester!"

"She is awake, Kingsley," said Nansie, lifting the baby from the cradle and putting her into his arms.

"This is a great joy to me," he said; "I really think she knows me; we shall be the best of friends. There is so much that is good in the world to show her—to teach her. Now, you and I together, love, will resolve to do our duty by her, and to do all that is in our power to make her happy."

CHAPTER XII.

An hour later, when Mr. Loveday returned home, Nansie, who had been listening for his footsteps, went out to meet him. Even in the dark he, with love's keen sight, observed that something of a pleasant nature had occurred.

"Good news, Nansie?"

"Speak low, uncle. Yes, good news. He has come home."

"Kingsley?"

"Yes, uncle. He is asleep with the baby by his side. He is very, very tired."

"How did it happen? How did he find you out?"

"It must have been almost by chance. I

was out making some little purchases, when I suddenly heard a voice behind me saying, quite naturally: 'It is Nansie!' Turning, I saw him, not clearly at first, because I was almost blind with joy. You must be very gentle with him, uncle."

"I will, my dear; but there is something in your voice—gentle for any especial reason?"

"Yes, for a special reason, which you will more fully discover for yourself. I am glad that I have seen you before he meets you; it will be better that you should be prepared."

"Prepared for what, my dear?"

"Kingsley is labouring under an impression that he has been away from us but a very short time. What *we* know to be real *he* believes to be fancies. He has made no reference to his travels abroad with Mr. Seymour, nor to the railway accident in which he was injured. He speaks of dreams, and even then not clearly. It is difficult for me to make myself understood——"

"Not at all, Nansie; I think I understand. The accident he met with has affected his memory; but it is good that he is with us now. We can take care of him, we can nurse him back to strength and health."

"How kind you are, uncle! Never thinking of yourself!"

"Nonsense, my dear, nonsense! It is entirely of myself that I am thinking, for I would not lose you and your dear ones for all the money the world contains. That is putting a small value upon money, though. I wish we had a little."

In his mind was the thought: "We need it all the more now," but he did not give the thought utterance.

"Is he low-spirited, despondent, Nansie?"

"No, uncle, quite the contrary. He is as light-hearted and gay as ever, and speaks in the same sweet, hopeful strains of the future, his anticipations of which led him into the error of——"

She stopped short; she did not complete the sentence. Her uncle completed it for her.

"Of marrying you, my dear. Do not regret it; accept it as a blessing, as it really is. Short-sighted mortals as we are to so constantly forget that life is short, and that its sweetest happiness is to be found in self-sacrifice—even, Nansie, in suffering!"

They entered the room together, and found Kingsley awake. He rose when his eyes lighted upon Mr. Loveday, and, with a bright smile, said:

"Nansie's uncle?"

"Yes, Kingsley," said Mr. Loveday.

And Nansie raised her uncle's hand to her lips, and kissed it in grateful recognition of the affectionate greeting.

"Now," said Kingsley, to whom strength seemed to have really returned; he held out his hand, and retained Mr. Loveday's in his as he spoke—"now what could be pleasanter, what could be brighter and more full of promise? Here, for the first time, we meet, and I recognise in you a friend. Believe me, sir, when I say a friend, it is said once and for ever; it is *meant* once and for ever. I am no butterfly, eh, Nansie?"

"No, dear Kingsley," she replied, pressing close to him.

He passed his arm round her.

"No butterfly," continued Kingsley, "except in the way of conversation, but that you will find out for yourself. I fly from one theme to another in the most inconsequential manner. A bad habit, sir, if it really meant anything serious, but it does not, and I have here by my side a spiritual support"—he kissed Nansie—"which never fails to recall me to the straight line at the precise and proper moment—as it does now; for looking at her, I am reminded of all we owe to you. Let me thank you in our joint names. I will not say that I hope to live to repay the debt, because there are some debts which it is good never to repay, and this is one. It is sometimes most ungracious to deliberately cancel an obligation."

"The debt is on my side, Kingsley," said Mr. Loveday, greatly won by the returned wanderer's speech and manner. "Nansie has brightened my life."

"She could do no less," said Kingsley, in a tone of grave and tender affection, "to the life of any person who has the happiness to know her."

Upon the invitation of Mr. Loveday, who knew, now that Kingsley had joined them, that certain changes were necessary in their domestic arrangements, and that Nansie could more readily effect them if she were left alone, the two men went out for a stroll. They returned after an absence of a couple of hours, and Kingsley presented Nansie with a few simple flowers, saying as he did so: "Our honeymoon is not yet over, my love."

Presently Kingsley, who, it was apparent, needed repose, was induced to retire to his bed. No sooner had he laid his head upon the pillow, than he was fast asleep. Nansie and her uncle sat together in the adjoining room, and conversed in low tones.

"It is as you say," observed Mr. Loveday, "he appears to have no memory—that is, no absolute, dependable memory—of what has transpired from the time he left you. I have not directly questioned him, feeling that it might not lead to a good result, and that he is not yet strong enough to bear even a slight shock; but indirectly I threw out a veiled suggestion or two, and his responses have convinced me of his condition. He has a vague impression of a railway accident in which some person whom he knew was killed, and some person whom he knew was injured, but he does not associate either the one or the other directly with himself. You will not mind my mentioning something, my dear, because in our position there must be between us no concealment. Kingsley has no money, not a penny."

"It is as I expected, uncle; but how did you discover it? Did he say so?"

"No, my dear, it came when he paused before a woman who was selling flowers. He put his hands into his pockets, and was, I think, more perplexed than distressed. 'Now this is too bad,' he remarked, and I, divining, paid the woman for the flowers he selected. It is wonderful to me how, circumstanced as he is, he managed to make his way home."

"Providence directed him, and protected him," said Nansie, devoutly, "and will surely smooth the path before us."

"With all my heart I hope so," responded Mr. Loveday; "meanwhile, until the better fortune smiles upon us, we must work all the harder, and bring our best courage to bear upon the present."

Their conversation was interrupted by a gentle tapping at the door, and opening it, they saw Timothy Chance, who had a covered basket on his arm which he laid upon the floor, and then respectfully greeted Mr. Loveday and Nansie, who, however, would not be content with this, but shook hands heartily with him.

A word of explanation as to Timothy's movements will here be useful.

They had not seen him since within a fortnight of the fire which had plunged them so low. When he was convinced that there was no present hope of Mr. Loveday being able to re-establish his business, he had looked out for a situation in the immediate neighbourhood, in order that he might be near the friends to whom he was so devotedly attached. But his efforts were not successful; no situation presented itself which he could accept, and as he was driven by necessity, which knows no law, he was compelled to avail himself of an engagement in the country some fifteen miles away, which offered itself in the nick of time. What eventually transpired will be best related in his own words.

"You thought I'd forgotten you, sir," he said to Mr. Loveday.

"No, my lad, I did not think that. My thought was that you had not been fortunate, and that you kept away out of consideration for us."

"Thank you, sir. You have a happy way of saying things. True, too, because I was not very fortunate at first; but there has been a turn in the wheel."

"A good turn, Timothy, I hope?"

"It will prove so, sir, if I have a head upon my shoulders; always trusting that there are no more fires."

"Ah," said Mr. Loveday, "we have had enough of those experiences."

"Yes, that we have, sir," responded Timothy, gravely; "but what I say is, 'Never despair.' I have not neglected my studies, sir, and I can give you the Latin words, if you like—'nil desperandum.'"

Timothy said this proudly, and with a bright eye.

"Good lad," said Mr. Loveday. "It is not in you to despair, Timothy. You are the stuff that men are made of, and will run ahead of all of us."

"Never so far ahead, sir," said Timothy, wistfully, "that I shall lose sight of the best friends a poor boy ever had; but that sounds like boastfulness."

"Not at all, Timothy, not at all. You speak with as much modesty as resolution. This turn in the wheel, my lad—what kind of a turn?"

"I think, sir," said Timothy, with a gay laugh, "that you could guess in once."

Mr. Loveday glanced at the basket on the floor, and made a guess in merry mood, for Timothy's blithe spirits were contagious.

"Eggs, Timothy?"

"Yes, sir," said Timothy, laughing again; "you have guessed it in once—eggs. But before I tell you about it"—he turned to Nansie—"how is baby?"

"Thriving beautifully, Timothy," replied Nansie.

"May I see her?" he asked.

"Wait a moment," said Nansie, and she went to the inner room, where baby was lying in her cradle. Returning, she said: "Yes, you may see her; but you must be very quiet. Do not make the least noise, and don't be surprised at what you see. My dear husband is home."

A bright light came into Timothy's face.

"I am glad," he said, "for your sake and baby's."

He stepped softly into the bedroom, accompanied by Nansie, and stood in silence for a few moments, gazing affectionately at the sleeping child.

"May I kiss her?" he said.

"Yes, Timothy, but very, very softly."

With the gentleness of a woman he stooped and kissed the child, and then came back with Nansie to the sitting-room, closing the door softly behind him.

"Eggs, as you say, sir," he recommenced, taking up the business part of the conversation where it had broken off. "You know that I had to sell off my little stock of fowls here, so that I might get to the situation I heard of. It wasn't a very good one, and it wasn't a very bad one; I had to work hard, which is a thing I shall never complain of, and although, besides my grub, I got very little a week, I managed to save a little out of that. Well, sir, six weeks ago I had two laying hens, and there I was established again in a small way, doing business for myself outside the hours I had to work for my employer. Then came a bit of good fortune, the turn in the wheel I spoke of. Not far from my place lives a blacksmith, and to him I've been going of a night for a little while past, teaching him to write a bit, teaching him to read a bit, and reading books to him myself that made him laugh and cry. He gets fond of me and we get talking together, especially about eggs. Says I, 'There's a fortune in eggs.' Says he, 'Is there?' Says I, 'No doubt of it.' And three weeks ago— that is, you know, three weeks after I had set up in business again with my two fowls —I put it all down in figures one night, and we went into it seriously. 'It seems all right,' says he. 'It is all right,' says I. 'Supposing you have not made a mistake,' says he, ' and that you are not being deceived by sparks.' He was hammering away on his anvil, and the sparks were flying up. 'Supposing that,' says he, 'and they are very deceptive creatures—sparks—bright as stars one moment, dead as ghosts the next, how much would it take to start the business?' 'First,' says I, 'there's the ground.' 'I've got that,' says he, 'at the back of the forge; an acre and a half.' 'Then,' says I, 'there's timber for fowl-houses, say enough for thirty to commence with.' 'I've got that,' says he, 'lying idle on the waste ground behind.' 'And nails you've got,' says I. You see, sir, I was speaking with confidence, and rather boldly, because a voice was whispering to me, 'Here's your chance, Timothy.' 'And tools to work nails and timber with,' says I. 'Labour will cost nothing; I should be carpenter and builder.' 'Should you?' says he, 'and I could give you a hand. But an acre and a half of ground and any amount of timber and nails won't lay eggs. Come to the grip—how much money to bring that about?" '£10 will be ample,' says I. 'I've got that,' says he, 'and more at the back of it. Say £10 then.' 'Do you mean it?' says I, my heart almost jumping out of my body. 'I never say what I don't mean,' says he, 'though I don't always say what I do. It is agreed, Timothy, that we go into partnership; rent of ground to be reckoned, nails and tools to be reckoned, timber to be reckoned, and £10 to be reckoned, as the capital of the firm. The sooner you start, the better.' I think you know enough of me, sir," continued Timothy, glowing, "to know that I didn't waste an hour. Waste an hour! I didn't waste a minute; and before that week was over the fowl-houses were up, not far away from the forge—because warmth, sir, is good for laying hens—and there was a stock of thirty black Hamburgs to start with. Now, sir and Mrs. Manners, we have been in business just one fortnight, and everything is going on swimmingly. My partner says he never saw such fowls, and says I deal in magic; but the only thing I deal in, sir, is common sense. So, being fairly started on my way, and having something good to tell, I burned to come and tell it to the friends I honour most; and now I must go. I have to get back to-night; but perhaps you will let me come to see you again."

"Indeed, we shall be delighted to see you at any time, Timothy," said Nansie, for he looked at her for an answer. "No one is more rejoiced at your good fortune, and at the prospect before you, than ourselves."

"I know that," said Timothy. "Good night, and God bless you."

"Your basket, Timothy," said Mr. Loveday.

"Oh, if you will excuse me, sir, it is yours, and not mine. I have bought it for you, and I hope you will not take it amiss." And off Timothy went, without another word.

Opening the basket when he was gone, they took out a score of new-laid eggs and a young fowl trussed for roasting. Tears came into Nansie's eyes.

"Did I not say, uncle," she murmured, "that Providence will smooth the path before us?"

CHAPTER XIII.

The week that followed was one of great anxiety to Nansie, springing less from the pecuniary circumstances of their position than from the state of Kingsley's health. The privations and the sufferings he had endured told upon him now that the excitement of the reunion with his wife was over, and for some days he was too weak to leave the house. He himself made light of his sickness, and would not admit that there was anything seriously the matter with him. They made no endeavour to impress this upon him, but he gathered it from the evidences of care and attention by which he was surrounded.

There was in the neighbourhood a doctor of great skill, who could have practised successfully in fashionable quarters at high fees, but who had deliberately chosen to remain among the poor, whom he loved and attended to with as much devotion as he would have displayed to the highest in the land. His fee was fixed at a shilling; when this was not forthcoming he was content with sixpence, and in many cases with nothing, making no complaints against tardy debtors. This man was always cheerful, ready, and willing, at whatever hour of the day or night; and, without ostentation, he played the part of a true minister to those who needed it most. It is pleasant to be able to limn, even thus briefly, the character of one in whose life and career were exhibited the noblest attributes of human nature. He and Mr. Loveday were friends, and shortly after Nansie came to live with her uncle Dr. Perriera was greatly attracted to her, no less by her gentle manners than by the display of attainments superior to those amongst whom she lived. When Mr Loveday was burnt out Dr. Perriera was the first to express sympathy with him; he would also have been the first to offer practical assistance had it not been that he was very poor, a fact which troubled him not at all so far as regarded himself, but frequently disturbed him when he came into contact with distress which it was not in his power to relieve. After the fire, when he attended Nansie of his own free will and prompting, he declined to receive any fee whatever, and to this Mr. Loveday did not demur.

As his name indicated, Dr. Perriera was of Spanish descent, and could, indeed, trace his genealogical record back to the days when Spain was first amongst the nations of the world in art, literature, and science. But the dark and heavy hand of bigotry effectually scotched the fair promise which lay before the favoured nation, and with the exodus of the Jews—to which race Dr. Perriera belonged—commenced the decay of a mighty nation.

On the day succeeding that of Kingsley's return Mr. Loveday called upon Dr. Perriera, and told him of it.

"I am greatly pleased," said Dr. Perriera; "it will be better medicine for Mrs. Manners than the finest drugs in the Pharmacopœia."

Then, in order that Dr. Perriera might be in possession of all necessary information, Mr. Loveday made him acquainted with the particulars of Kingsley's association with Mr. Seymour, following those up with the intelligence of the strange hallucination under which Kingsley was labouring with respect to his long absence from home. To Mr. Loveday's surprise, Dr. Perriera showed an intimate knowledge of the movements of the so-called Mr. Seymour, as well as of the secret societies in the interests of which it was said that he travelled.

"Of Mr. Manners," said Dr. Perriera, "I know nothing. In Mr. Seymour's transactions he was little better than a cipher, and was probably used as an innocent decoy, or as a means to avert suspicion from the doings of his chief."

"How have you become acquainted with these affairs," asked Mr. Loveday; "you, who seem to have no spare moments of time apart from your professional offices?"

"I have time and to spare for much." replied Dr. Perriera, smiling. "I keep up rather an extensive correspondence with many European societies which have for their object the advancement of science and humanity."

"Humanity!" exclaimed Mr. Loveday.

"I call it by that name," said Dr. Perriera. "Were it possible that the ends aimed at could be reached, the toilers of the world would be undoubtedly benefited. The advocated means are frequently pernicious and indefensible; but this occasionally arises from the fact that men of keen intellectual power are goaded to madness by the tyranny of old systems. However, enough of this; I think much but speak little of such matters. I have my small part to play in the world, as to the larger and grander movements of which I can simply look on and observe."

Dr. Perriera called to see Kingsley, and of his own accord visited him daily. He gave Nansie kindly hope and sympathy, but did not enter into the peculiarities of her husband's case. With Mr. Loveday he was more open.

"It is a singular condition," he said. "The loss of memory is not at all uncommon, nor, either, is its recovery; but in most instances this loss is a total loss, time, well-known incidents, relative circumstances, the names of friends and acquaintances, even one's own name, being plunged for a period into absolute obscurity. But here the loss of memory is partial, and the singular phase of it is that it affects only those circumstances of the past which it would be disagreeable to recall. He remembers all that is pleasant and happy in his life, but forgets all that has brought trouble upon him. It belongs to this phase that he is incapable of realising the privations of the life which seems to lie before him. His temperament is exceptionally bright and cheerful; he looks upon the happy side of nature, and every hopeful sentiment which passes his lips seems to blossom into flower at the moment of its utterance. I can imagine no happier condition of being; but in a poor man it has its grave and most serious side."

"How?" inquired Mr. Loveday.

"In the fact," replied Dr. Perriera, "that it allows no room for effort, that it affords no incentive to it, that it creates a sure contentment even for a crust of bread, and an utter obliviousness to what may be necessary for those who, he being the head of the family, are naturally dependent upon him."

"That is to say," observed Mr. Loveday, "that there is no hope of his being the bread-winner."

"None," said Dr. Perriera, "until there is a radical change in him; and I confess to being at a loss as to how this can be effected."

The correctness of the good doctor's diagnosis was verified by an incident which did not come to the ears of Nansie or her uncle until after its occurrence. Stronger in body, and able to walk abroad without assistance, Kingsley soon made himself acquainted with all the intricacies of the neighbourhood; and on a certain morning he wended his steps to the West-end of the city, and stood before his father's house. Without hesitation he knocked and rang, and upon the door being opened, pushed his way past the astonished servant, and walked straight to his father's study. There sat Mr. Manners, who gazed at his son with sternness and some inward agitation which he was successful in concealing.

"Good morning, father," said Kingsley, drawing a chair to the table, and seating himself; then glancing at the papers scattered about, added in a tone of inquiry: "Fresh contracts?"

Mr. Manners did not reply to the question.

"What brings you here?" he asked.

Kingsley had grown thinner since he last saw him, and that circumstance and the shabbiness of Kingsley's appearance suddenly inspired in the heart of Mr. Manners the hope that his son had come to him in submission.

"I was anxious about you, father," said Kingsley in an affectionate tone, "it seems so long since we saw each other. A son must not be forgetful of his duties."

"Ah," said Mr. Manners, his hope growing, "you recognise that at last?"

"At last!" said Kingsley, in a tone of cheerful surprise. "I have always recognised it. I cannot recall that I have ever been wanting in my duty to you."

Mr. Manners stared at his son, debating now within himself what kind of part Kingsley had come to play. There was a silence of a few moments, during which Kingsley gazed at the familiar objects of the room with great calmness, and quite at his ease.

"The object of your visit?" demanded Mr. Manners.

"I have told you, father. Are you well?"

"Yes, I am well."

"And happy?"

"Yes," replied Mr. Manners, setting his teeth, "and happy. That knowledge will hurt you, perhaps."

"Why, no, father, it delights me. Everything, as usual, prospers with you, of course."

"Everything, as usual, prospers with me," said Mr. Manners, mechanically. "Did you inquire of the servant if I was at home?"

"No, why should I? It was my home once as well as yours."

"But is no longer," said Mr. Manners, with a deepening frown.

"Oh, well, no, in a certain sense," said Kingsley, "not directly, but indirectly still my home as well as yours. There are ties which can never be broken, and which you, in the goodness of your heart, would never wish to be broken. I should not like to hear from any man's lips that you think otherwise; I am afraid I should say something unpleasant to him."

Kingsley's cordial manner and cheerful voice would have mystified most men with a weaker order of mind than Mr. Manners';

but although this was not the case with the great contractor, he was certainly at a loss to account for them. He knew that Kingsley possessed a soul of frankness and honesty, and he could not readily bring himself to believe that it was cunning and duplicity which had induced his son to seek this interview. Still, for the exhibition of these qualities he would have been, as he always was with all men, perfectly prepared, but not for the ingenuousness with which he was now confronted. He thought to turn the tables upon Kingsley.

"Are you well?" he asked.

"Quite well, father," replied Kingsley.

"And happy?"

"Quite happy, father."

"And prosperous?"

"To be quite well and happy," said Kingsley, in no spirit of evasion, "is not that a prosperous state?"

"You are quibbling with me," said Mr.

Manners, "and I am not in the mood, and have no time for trifling."

"I shall not detain you long, father; you have eased my mind, and I shall go away presently, quite contented. As to quibbling, you, who know me so well and have been so good to me, must know that I am incapable of such conduct."

"I decline to argue with you. Come to the point at once. You wish to make some kind of appeal to me. I did hope that you had come in submission."

"I have, father; submission in all things that accord with one's duty."

"With your duty to me?"

"To you and to others who are dear to me."

"I will not listen," said Mr. Manners, "to anything concerning them."

"I will not force it upon you. There shall be nothing discordant between us. But what do you mean by 'appeal'?"

"You are here to ask for money, as those who have separated us have been here before you."

"Indeed you are quite wrong. There has been, there shall be, no separation between us. I love you as I have always done, as I always shall love you. And they appealed to you for money! Did you give it to them?"

"No, nor will I to you."

"Oh, but I need none. You have been since my earliest remembrance most liberal to me, but you cannot accuse me of being mercenary. I should like you to know my wife, I should like you to know and love our child. If you are too busy for that now, we will wait; when you visit us, which surely you will do some day, you will be pleased at the manner in which we shall receive you; all the honour that is due to you shall be cheerfully rendered."

"This mockery must end," said Mr.

Manners; "go! But before you leave, it will, perhaps, be as well for me to say what is in my mind."

"Yes, father," said Kingsley, gently.

"I do not know," said Mr. Manners, in a set hard tone, "whether I should ever have been inclined to forgive your disobedience and undutifulness; I do not know, after what has passed, whether, you being my son upon whom once all my hopes were centred, I should have been disposed to once more hold out my hand to you. I think it would not have been possible, but there may have been, at least, some remote chance of a partial reconciliation. If there was such a chance, you have utterly destroyed it by your conduct during the past few months."

"What conduct do you refer to?" asked Kingsley, smiling. "You surely are labouring under some delusion!"

"It is no delusion," said Mr. Manners, "that you have been travelling for some time with a person of infamous character and designs!"

"Surely it must be, father. Does the man live? If he does, he will disprove it."

"I will fall in with your humour," said Mr. Manners, "and will pay no attention to your amazing evasions; all the more amazing, all the more inexcusable, when adopted towards a man like myself. Do you pretend that you are unacquainted with the person who travelled under the name of Seymour? Do you pretend that travelling in close association with him as you did for so long a time, you had no connection with the designs he was wishful to promote?"

"You remind me strangely," replied Kingsley, "of something which has been troubling me—no, I am wrong in saying troubling me, I mean that has been interesting me. There have undoubtedly been some such designs as you refer to, mysterious and inexplicable enough to me, but the interesting part of the matter is, how did it ever come into my mind that I could have been associated with them? Clearly, I must have evolved the idea out of a too vivid imagination, because I cannot trace the slightest actual connection between me and them. Similarly, too, with the name you have mentioned — Seymour. How did it come into my mind that I knew such a gentleman? Clearly, he must have existed; and now there occurs to me a dim remembrance of a railway accident in which a gentleman of the name of Seymour was killed, and many were injured. How comes the knowledge of that circumstance to me? May I not also have evolved that from my imagination? Anyway, I shall not allow myself to be troubled by matters which I cannot directly trace, though I cannot avoid being interested in them. But what you have said has another bearing, as though I had done something to disgrace my name.

Of course, such a thing would be impossible, and if I am indebted to any ill-natured person for having aroused in you any suspicion to my hurt, I make him my hearty acknowledgments without bearing the slightest ill-will against him, because after all, father, a serious calumny should not be allowed to have weight unless an absolute foundation of fact can be brought forward, as cannot be done in my case. Man must be judged by his own actions, not by what people say of him. You infer that this Mr. Seymour travelled to promote infamous designs with which you suppose me to be in sympathy. What designs, father?"

"Republicanism," said Mr. Manners, not displeased at being brought to the point, "Socialism, Communism, and the overthrow of existing institutions which are a blessing to mankind."

"Ah, but there, you know," said Kingsley, with no departure from his light mood, "you open up debatable matter. It is not disagreeable to me. I was always fond of argument, although I have been accused of too freely wandering away from one upon the slightest excuse. You condemn Republicanism, but I think I would sooner live under a Republic than a Monarchy."

"What you say confirms the accusation I and others bring against you."

"Not at all. I am merely expressing my view of a large matter. You see, father, there is so much misery in the world, so much undeserved suffering, so much compulsory poverty, such astounding inequalities in the social condition of the people, that a fair-minded man cannot possibly avoid wishing to remedy these ills. What are you touching the bell for?"

"For the servant to show you to the door."

"I do not need him; I know my way out. Your time is valuable, and it is inconsiderate of me to take up so much of it. Is my mother in?"

"No."

"I am sorry; I wished to see her. She is well, I hope."

"Quite well. She has not a sorrow in the world. And now, for the last time, leave the room—and the house."

His peremptory harsh tone had no effect upon Kingsley, who, with a genial nod and a "Good morning, father," left the house with a light step.

In the evening he informed Nansie and Mr. Loveday of his visit to his father, and to their astonishment described it as one of a pleasant character. Their astonishment was all the greater when they read a letter which was delivered personally to Kingsley. It was from a firm of lawyers, and was written in accordance with instructions received from Mr. Manners. In the first place it conveyed an intimation that Kingsley would not be allowed again to enter his father's house; in the second place it contained a warning that if he made any further endeavour to force himself into his father's presence, proceedings would be taken against him for the trespass.

"I think," said Kingsley, "that lawyers must have been invented expressly to torment mankind; they never can put a thing pleasantly. My father, I suppose, is too busy to write to me himself, so he told his lawyers to do so, and they, wishing to make things as unpleasant as possible, send me a communication couched in terms which my father would certainly resent. Of course I shall not go to him again until he sends for me."

So saying he tore up the letter and put it into the fire.

A few days afterwards it was announced in the papers that Mr. Manners had broken up his London establishment, and with his wife and his nephew, Mr. Mark Inglefield, had started on a foreign tour, which was likely to be of long duration. This paragraph was read by Kingsley, and caused in him the first spark of resentment he had exhibited since his return.

"I am sorry," he said, "that my father has taken up with such a man as Mark Inglefield. He is dangerous and cold-blooded, and I am afraid no friend of mine. Not that I want him for a friend, but that, being with my father, he may say something against us. However, to use your dear mother's saying, Nansie: 'Everything will come right in the end.'"

With this comfortable assurance he dismissed the matter from his mind, as was his habit.

And here the course of our story renders it necessary that the curtain shall fall for a certain time. When it rises again seventeen years will have passed away.

CHAPTER XIV.

BEFORE, however, we join the threads which link the past with the present, we will briefly glance through the years during which Nansie's and Kingsley's daughter grew into the beautiful springtime of young maidenhood, and before whom fair visions rose even in the midst of surroundings pernicious enough to poison the sweetest dreams. They poison many, and the awaking would be sad and bitter were the home influences with which they were from their birth familiar of a purer and more refining nature. In judging them we judge them from our standpoint instead of theirs, and we too often condemn where we should pity. In respect of these influences Nansie's home shone forth a sweet and bright example of what may be accomplished when the early training is good. There were few poorer homes than Nansie's, there were few lives more full of struggle, but she kept herself and those most dear to her pure through all the bitter phases of the battle she was destined to fight. She worked hard, and taxed her strength to the utmost, but she never complained, least of all to or of her husband, who should by right have been the bread-winner. The greatness of the sacrifice he had made for her had, as we have seen, deeply impressed her. At first, it is true, the heavenly glamour of true love had wholly possessed her, but even then, had she known what she learnt when it was too late, she would not have accepted the sacrifice, though her heart had been broken. Indeed, in those never-to-be-forgotten days the actual responsibility lay not with her. Kingsley made so light of the difference in their social positions, and she was so entirely guided by him whom she regarded as the king of men, that she had no idea of the extent of his father's wealth or of the difficulties in their way. Had she been aware of these, not alone her love for Kingsley but her practical good sense and self-respect would have effectually directed her not to yield to his implorings. But these hidden from her, she followed the dictates of her heart. All the more devoted and considerate towards him was she when she learnt the truth; all the more noble did his conduct appear in her eyes. If reproach lay at either door, it lay at hers; if either of them had the right to complain, it was he. In the early days of their union she had discovered that he was deficient in those qualities which are necessary to fight the hard battle of life even with moderate success. Should she blame him for this? What right had she to do so? He had not deceived her, and his prospects and education had not been of a nature to render him fit for the cruel battle. All the more was he to be pitied; all the more need was there that she should show him the tenderest consideration. And she did so. Willingly did she take upon her own shoulders the burden of the struggle, and worked cheerfully and willingly with heaviest odds against her. From the effects of the railway accident he never recovered, and his memory never returned to him. Although he did little to help the home, his gentleness, his contentment with a crust, his light-heartedness, brightened it. And so they went on to middle age, with a full measure of love to lighten their lot.

CHAPTER XV.

At the end of seventeen years we renew our acquaintance with the personages who play their part in this story; but before they are re-introduced it will be pertinent to touch upon certain political changes which had taken place in the social condition of the people during this period. The growth of these changes had been going on for a great number of years, and the seeds may be said to have been sown with the advent of the cheap press. A slow growth at first, the slender roots beneath the soil having scarcely strength to take firm hold; but as they became stronger they became bolder, and were now winding themselves firmly and stoutly around the roots of old institutions which, fixed as they had been for centuries, were in this audacious grasp beginning to show signs of weakness and decay. There was a time when what is known as the higher classes would have regarded as incredibly monstrous the idea of affinity between them and those who moved in the lower grooves. There was a time when the lower classes themselves would have regarded as the height of effrontery the idea of raising their eyes in any other than a timid way to the higher classes who ruled and dominated them. That time is past, never to be revived. There exist here and there in England instances of feudalism almost as marked as any that can be drawn from the time that is gone. In those places the high hand is still employed to destroy any hope of progress among the people, but these instances are rare, and are becoming still rarer. The penny newspaper has drawn prince and peasant, noble and serf—for we have the latter even in free England—closer together, and have taught the multitude that all men and women are human alike, and that there exists in the upper grades no divine right of power and supremacy. And strangely enough, it is through this very means that the higher classes have been forced to recognise the power and the might of the lower. This new condition of things has also been promoted by other causes than the advancement of intelligence. The increase of population has forced upon reasoning minds among the people the inevitable necessity of radical changes in the hitherto existing order of things; and the scarecrow of vested interests, which is set up by those who lay claim to them, will be powerless to check the onward march. There are, unhappily, retarding influences, springing from the very vices of the people, which prove stumbling-blocks in every step that is taken or suggested. But for these vices the victims themselves are scarcely to blame. It is not an inherent matter, it is a matter of birth whether one grows up with the courtly airs of St. James' or with the degrading characteristics of St. Giles'; and it is good to observe that there are statesmen in St. James' who recognise the fact, and who are working honestly and earnestly towards a better end —or rather, not to speak paradoxically, towards a better beginning. And yet, despite these reflections, society perhaps never laboured under greater ills than at present. The ephemeral, vicious fashions of St. James' were never in greater vogue than now; the cunning and vices of St. Giles' were never more conspicuous and apparent. There was a time when much of this, both in the higher and lower classes, was hidden, but in the present day everything is brought to light in the conflict of testimony which a fair-minded survey is forced to perceive. There are cogent and powerful arguments to be adduced in justification by each side against the other, but these are small meandering rivulets which but slightly affect the rolling of the grand tide. Out of this seeming chaos good must come. It is, as it has ever been, still the fashion of the age—even now that darkness no longer weighs heavily upon it—to shift and evade a responsibility. Thus, the owner of a great landed estate, in portions of which hotbeds of vice and misery can be found, is in the habit of shrugging his shoulders when public attention is directed to them, and of saying in effect: "It is not my affair, it is the affair of my agents." But this attitude, which springs either from fear, cowardice, or indifference, can no longer be accepted. It is the owner alone who is responsible; it is the owner and the owner alone, who thrives and fattens upon these systems, who is in justice accountable for the evils of which he is undoubtedly the breeder; and the attitude he assumes proves him to be unfitted for his responsibilities. The remedy is his to apply, and if he apply it not in time the power of doing so will be taken out of his hands. The present opportunity is his; the future with its dark possibilities lies before him. It is well if he take heed of this before it is too late. Let us present an illustration bearing upon our story.

Two years after Kingsley's return, Nansie and her uncle, who constituted the government of ways and means of the household, decided that the rooms they occupied were too dear; they paid for these rooms five shillings a week. They looked out for others, and decided upon two rooms at the top of a house in a narrow court, in comparison with which Church Alley was a paradise. This court was so narrow that the occupants of the houses on either side could hold conversation with each other from opposite windows. The rooms were very small, the ceilings very low, the ventilation horrible, the sanitary arrangements disgraceful—a description of affairs which renders it all the more wonderful how Nansie's daughter, Hester, and how Nansie herself, could have kept themselves pure and sweet in an atmosphere so inimical to healthful moral and physical growth. The court — with other thoroughfares as narrow and stunted and vicious in its immediate neighbourhood— was built upon part of an estate which belonged to a family the head of which sat in the House of Lords. There was in the house in which Nansie resided a cellar, politely called a basement. In this cellar were two rooms—one back, one front. The back room had a fireplace, but no window; what light filtered into it was filtered through a pane of glass let into the compartment which divided it from the front room, and as this front room itself could boast of but one window, the light it supplied to its neighbour was of a character so dismal and forlorn as scarcely to relieve the darkness into which, by the laws of its structure, it was plunged. But, indeed, to call it by the name of light was the bitterest of mockeries, not alone because of the small play it had, but because of the dust and cobwebs which covered both sides of the pane of glass. In this back room, however, lived a family of father, mother, and three children, all pigging together—there is no other word to describe it—in the narrow space which may fitly be likened to the Black Hole of Calcutta. They had certainly one advantage—that they could run out when they pleased and breathe the fœtid air of the court, and thence into wider thoroughfares where the air was not vile enough to poison them. Had this opportunity not been theirs they would have died in a week. The social station of the head of this family was that of a scavenger, for six months of the year out of work. His wife occasionally got half a day's washing to do; the children were young and helpless, and the life they all lived can be more easily imagined than described. To describe it faithfully would be impossible in the pages or columns of any respectable journal, the details were so frightful and vile. And it is in no class spirit, in no spirit but that of mournfulness and amazement, that the fact is repeated—that the virtual owner of this back cellar sat in the House of Lords.

The front room of the cellar was occupied by a cobbler. The window which supplied light to his room was a practicable one, resembling a shutter of glass which could be put up and taken down at will; and during the whole of the year, in fair weather or foul—except upon those occasions, which were frequent enough, when he was drunk—the man could be seen by passers-by plying his thread and awl. Fortunately for himself and for everybody about him, he was a bachelor.

There were two rooms on the ground-floor, the front occupied by a "baked-tater man," his wife, and two young children. At those periods of the year when baked potatoes with their seasoning of pepper and salt were not in request, the man, being a strict Conservative, was idle, allowing his wife to accompany a friend of his, who drove quite a roaring trade in fairly good neighbourhoods with his barrow of seasonable flowers. For this labour she was paid in coin one shilling a day, and a share of his bread and cheese or bread and meat, as well as of the sundry pots of beer his thirsty soul demanded in his peregrinations. Their two children played in the gutters, being not exceptional in this respect, because most of the children in the court found in the gutters a veritable Crystal Palace of delights.

The back room on the ground-floor was occupied by a large family—father, mother, and seven children — all employed from morning till night, and often from night till morning, upon the manufacture of match-boxes, at the rate of twopence three-farthings a gross. Their united earnings never exceeded fifteen shillings, often were less. Thus the grim effort to make both ends meet, no less than their close and long hours of toil, rendered them white, pinched, haggard-looking, and almost fleshless.

On the first-floor front lived a married couple with an only child. The man had once been a law-writer, probably not a very skilful or capable scribe, seeing he had never been able to save a penny. However, it was here he found himself plunged into poverty's depths and unable to follow his calling, the muscles of his right hand being paralysed. The wife had become a shirt-maker, and was assisted by her child, a girl of sixteen. Neither of these was a skilful workwoman, and after the payment of their rent there was seldom left at the end of the week more than seven or eight shillings to expend in food.

The first-floor back was tenanted by a widow with two children, twins, a little more than a year old. Being unable to find any other means of living she had, by force of circumstances, drifted into the rear ranks of the ballet, where she helped to fill the stage on a salary of two shillings a night. Commencing late in life to learn to dance, there was for her no hope of promotion in the ranks. Her lot was hard enough, Heaven knows; but she would have found it harder, because of the impossibility of leaving her babies every night for a good many hours together, had it not been for the kindness of the law-writer's wife and daughter, who often looked after them when the mother was absent.

In the rooms on the second floor, which were very small attics with slanting roofs, lived Nansie, Kingsley, and their daughter.

Mr. Loveday took his meals with them, but slept elsewhere. The front attic was used as a living-room during the day, and as a bedroom during the night—the shut-up bedstead being sometimes occupied by Kingsley alone and sometimes by Hester. Altogether there slept in this small house twenty-eight persons. The frontage of the house was twelve feet, its depth twenty feet; and it will be gathered from these dimensions how utterly unsuitable it was in the way of health and morals for so large a number of occupants. In this respect, anything more vicious can scarcely be imagined, and yet this house was but one of many built upon land owned by an enormously wealthy man, one who helped to make laws for the social regeneration of the people. Were the facts forced upon his knowledge in the way of accusation, he would doubtless plead ignorance of the circumstances, as others have pleaded before him; but this convenient blindness to the truth will not serve; this convenient shifting of responsibility is of no avail; an unfaithful steward he has been, and an unfaithful steward he remains.

CHAPTER XVI.

It was a great night at the Wilberforce Club, and the members mustered in force. Numbers were unable to obtain admission, and the spaces outside the room in which the club held its meetings were thronged by working men and lads, many of them members of the Wilberforce. These, although disappointed at being shut out, did not give vent to their feelings in the shape of grumbling, but good-humouredly accepted the position, and split themselves into convenient knots for the purposes of discussion.

The Wilberforce was a working man's club, similar in its nature and aims to the numerous institutions of a like character which exist in the centres of labour in all the great towns and cities of the kingdom. It commenced with small beginnings, the original number of members being twelve, who met weekly at the lodgings of one or the other for the purpose of discussing political matters affecting themselves. A very short time passed before others made application to be allowed to join the band of twelve, and then the idea was formed of organising a working man's club, to be called the Wilberforce. The originator of this movement was a man of strong opinions, by trade a carpenter. He was a ready orator, and he ruled over his followers by force of this gift, as well as by the superior knowledge he possessed of the movements of the age in which he lived. It may not be uninteresting to place upon record a report of the meeting at which the club may have said to have been born.

By consent of a licensed victualler it was

held in a room in the "Three Jolly Butcher Boys," a noted public-house in the neighbourhood. There were some thirty persons present, all humble, earnest, hard-working labourers in different crafts. Mr. Bartholomew, the carpenter and initiator of the movement, elected himself into the chair.

"We are only a scattered body as yet," he said, "and none of us has the proper authority to propose and second a chairman, so by your leave——" He moved to the head of the table and seated himself. Drawing out his two-foot rule he used it as a mace to rap the table.

"A dozen of us," he said, rising to his feet when all the others were seated and silent, "have been meeting for a little while past at one place and another, with a notion that opening our minds to each other wouldn't do any harm. That has been proved; it has done good. There ain't one of the dozen who don't understand the rights and wrongs of things better than he did before. Now, this was no hole and corner affair, and as it's got about, and as there's a wish of a good many others to join us, why, I say, 'Join us and welcome.'"

There was a murmur of approval, and a general rapping of knuckles and scraping of feet on the part of the original eleven.

"The more the merrier, I say," continued Mr. Bartholomew. "What we are working for, or what we are going to work for, is the general good of all alike — in a fair way, mind! Nothing wrong, nothing violent——"

"Hear, hear," from the auditors.

"Everything constitutional. When my wife doesn't agree with me, I don't knock her down, as brutes do—I argue with her; if that don't make her agree with me, I keep on arguing with her; and if she's that obstinate that she won't agree with me even then, I go on arguing with her; and the upshot of it is that I fairly wear her down, and in the end she's bound to agree with me."

Murmurs of approval and a little laughter from the audience, with here and there a *sotto-voce* remark: "Bartholomew knows what he's about."

"Now," pursued Mr. Bartholomew, "that's what I call constitutional. I don't mean to say that I ain't open to conviction myself, but when a man knows he's right, all that he's got to do is to go ahead—always in a constitutional way. Now there's the Government—it's right, or it's wrong. If it's right, let it remain as it is; if it's wrong, it's got to be altered."

"It's wrong, that's what it is," blurted out a working man.

"Not so fast, not so fast," said Mr. Bartholomew; "saying it's wrong don't make it so. We've got to find it out by argument and open minds, constitutionally, and that ain't a thing for to-night; and it ain't a thing that can be settled in a day, or a week, or a month, or a year. It'll take time, because—I don't mind confessing to you my opinion — that what's got to be done is no trifling matter; it's a mighty matter, mates, with kings, and queens, and princes, and princesses, and prime ministers, and chancellors of the exchequer, all mixed up in it. Do you know what I call those ladies and gentlemen, mates? I call them the frillings. The solid mass, the real body, is here." He gave the table a great thump with his fist.

"Bravo, Bartholomew!" from many voices. "We've got a man at the head of us!"

The excitement was beginning to rise.

"You ain't got anybody at the head of you. All that sort of thing—forming ourselves into an institution, election of officers, and so on—has got to be done. We're just then, I go on arguing with her; and the upshot of it is that I fairly wear her down, and in the end she's bound to agree with me."

Murmurs of approval and a little laughter from the audience, with here and there a *sotto-voce* remark: "Bartholomew knows what he's about."

"Now," pursued Mr. Bartholomew, "that's what I call constitutional. I don't mean to say that I ain't open to conviction myself, but when a man knows he's right, all that he's got to do is to go ahead—always in a constitutional way. Now there's the Government—it's right, or it's wrong. If it's right, let it remain as it is; if it's wrong, it's got to be altered."

"It's wrong, that's what it is," blurted out a working man.

"Not so fast, not so fast," said Mr. Bartholomew; "saying it's wrong don't make it so. We've got to find it out by argument and open minds, constitutionally, and that ain't a thing for to-night; and it ain't a thing that can be settled in a day, or a week, or a month, or a year. It'll take time, because—I don't mind confessing to you my opinion — that what's got to be done is no trifling matter; it's a mighty matter, mates, with kings, and queens, and princes, and princesses, and prime ministers, and chancellors of the exchequer, all mixed up in it. Do you know what I call those ladies and gentlemen, mates? I call them the frillings. The solid mass, the real body, is here." He gave the table a great thump with his fist.

"Bravo, Bartholomew!" from many voices. "We've got a man at the head of us!"

The excitement was beginning to rise.

"You ain't got anybody at the head of you. All that sort of thing—forming ourselves into an institution, election of officers, and so on—has got to be done. We're just of uttering this small word which caused general laughter—"I blame ourselves. I was saying that every man has the regulation number of limbs and members, the regulation measure of appetite, the regulation instincts, sentiments, and all that sort of thing, and I was going to say when I was interrupted that you'll find something in Coriolanus about the stomach which rather bears upon the point. I dare say there are one or two in the room who'll remember my mentioning this at a meeting before the last general election, when I spoke against the Conservative candidate. It was a Conservative meeting, and the hall was pretty well packed with one-siders, but the candidate—a gentleman, mates—got me a fair hearing, and I was listened to. Yes, you were there, and you"—pointing to two in the room who nodded gravely. "Well, when I'd done about this Coriolanus and the stomach business, up gets the Conservative candidate and says: 'I don't for a moment doubt that our good friend, Mr. Bartholomew'—he knew my name; I handed it up to him on paper, not having an engraved card——"

"Ha! ha! ha!" from the back of the room.

Mr. Bartholomew looked severely in that direction, and said:

"What are you ha! ha! ha-ing about? Do you think I want to make a point against gentlemen who carry cards? You're mistaken, though perhaps I too was wrong in the way I put it. 'I don't for a moment doubt,' said the Conservative candidate, 'that our good friend, Mr. Bartholomew, who I hope one day will blossom into a good Conservative'—between you and me, mates, that will be never."

"Hear, hear."

"'I don't for a moment doubt that he is right about what he says of Coriolanus and the application of it. I don't remember the lines myself, but I will take them from him, and I will give him an answer in an anecdote. There was a serpent once, a regulation serpent, a twining, slimy, creeping, crawling reptile, with head, and tail, and all other necessary parts. Now, Mr. Bartholomew knows that it is a law of nature for serpents that in going through life the head goes first. I don't know exactly how old the serpent was when its tail ranged itself upon what I may call the opposition side. It said to the head: "Look here, I ain't going to be dragged about in this manner all day long, and all night long, just where you like to take me. I won't stand it. It's *my* turn for an innings; fair play is fair play." All the other parts of the serpent joined in the argument, and the tail was so noisy and blustering that it carried along with it every bit of the serpent but the head. Now, it unfortunately happened,' said the Conservative candidate, 'that this particular head of this particular serpent was weak-minded; anyhow, it was foolish enough to say: "Put it to the vote, and I'll stand by it. You shall decide who goes first, the tail or me." It was put to the vote, and it was decided by a large majority that the tail was right, and that it ought to have an innings. "Very well," says the head, "I resign." Then the tail, crying, "Come along," took command. But, my friends,' said the Conservative candidate, 'you don't need to be told — though perhaps it will enlighten Mr. Bartholomew—that the eyes of a serpent's body are in its head, and not in its tail, and that as the tail dragged its way along it couldn't see where it was going. It got into a prickly hedge, and when the other portions of the body felt the sting and the pain they cried out: "What are you about?" "Oh, that's nothing," answered the tail, working its way out of the prickly hedge, "I am new to the business, that's all; you must put up with a mistake or two—that's only fair, you know." "Yes, yes," said the other parts of the body; "go on, go on." He did, and came to a part of the forest where there was a smouldering fire. Straight into this fire crept the tail, and, maddened with pain, crept farther into it, hoping to escape, and in less than no time the tail and the other rebellious parts of the body were burnt to ashes. The head alone remained.'"

Mr. Bartholomew paused for a moment or two, and then said:

"I see some of you fidgeting at your pipes. Fill 'em and smoke 'em. We're not regularly formed, and whether we shall always be at liberty to smoke while we're talking is a matter for you to settle by-and-by."

The pipes being filled and lighted, Mr. Bartholomew went on.

"That was the story the Conservative

candidate told, and it set the packed meeting cheering and laughing to that degree that I couldn't get in another word, and was supposed to be settled. But the Conservative candidate made a great many serious mistakes in that illustration. He intended to liken the Government of England, and everybody else in it, to one single being, whether it was beast, bird, or fish don't matter, because it won't do, mates, because it doesn't apply. True enough there must be a head to all constituted societies, to all forms of government, but, mates——"

And here the speaker rested his two hands upon the table and bent earnestly forward.

"We who are governed have eyes; we're not like the serpent's tail—we can see where we're going. The road is stretched before us, and our eyes are open. The serpent's tail not only had no eyes, he had no brains—we have, and we can judge. The serpent's tail not only had no eyes and no brains, it had no heart—we have, and we can see, and judge, and love, and suffer, and enjoy with as large a capacity as those who govern us. I don't for one moment believe that the view the Conservative candidate took—he didn't get in, you know, mates——"

"Ha, ha, ha!" from the audience.

"Is the view entertained by the Conservative party, the leading members of which are far too sensible and clever to put forward such narrow-minded theories. But it must never be forgotten that they're in the main looking out more for themselves, and for their own interests, than for us and ours. That's human nature, and I don't complain of it; if I did, it would be in a measure like cutting the ground from under our own feet, because one of the objects of this meeting — the principal object, I may say — is to look after ourselves and our own interests, which we've got the idea has been rather lost sight of. Now, before I come to the wind up of my speech — it has been a great deal longer than I intended to make it——"

"Not a bit too long, Bart," was the general cry.

"Much obliged, mates. Before I come to the end of it, I want to impress one thing upon you. All over the world there are to be found men who go in for equality, with a capital E. Some of those men are scholars, lots of 'em clever and talented; but, mates, they've got a warp in their minds. Such a thing as equality ain't possible. If it was possible to establish it at nine o'clock tonight, by nine o'clock to-morrow morning it wouldn't exist. There must be different degrees among human beings, there must be inequalities, like the very world we live in, which, as we've been taught in school, resembles the outside of an orange. But our argument is—because I suppose we're pretty well agreed upon it—that the inequalities are now too great, and require to be rubbed down a bit. It's a difficult question, and it's got to be treated with good sense. And now, thanking you for your attention, and the meeting being regularly opened, we'll proceed to business."

Mr. Bartholomew sat down amid a volley of applause, after which there was a long silence, he being really the only practical man among them; or, to speak more correctly, the only man who had practice in this kind of movement, and knew how to conduct it.

"The first thing we've got to do, you know," he said, looking around, " is to propose a resolution forming ourselves into a distinct body. As the chairman of the meeting I can't propose any resolution; it is for one of you to do it."

"All right, chairman," said a bold boot and shoemaker, "I do it."

"What?" inquired Mr. Bartholomew.

"Propose it," said the bold boot and shoemaker.

"Propose what?" asked Mr. Bartholomew.

"That we're a distinct body," said the bold boot and shoemaker.

"I seconds it," said another boot and shoemaker, starting up, and sinking instantly into his chair, covered with confusion. It was the first public speech he had ever made.

"No, no, that won't do," said Mr. Bartholomew, "you must put it in words—understandable words. You propose that we form ourselves into a working man's club. That's your proposition, ain't it?"

"That's it," said the bold boot and shoemaker.

"And you second it," said Mr. Bartholomew, looking at boot and shoemaker No. 2, who faintly nodded. He had not the courage to speak again.

"It is proposed by Mr. Richard Chappel," said Mr. Bartholomew, "boot and shoemaker, and seconded by Mr. William Blackmore, that we form ourselves into a working man's club, we being all of us Liberals, and our chief object being the political and social advancement of working men generally. Those in favour of the resolution signify it in the usual manner by holding up their hands."

Every hand was held up.

"On the contrary," said the chairman.

Full half of those present held up their hands.

"No, no, no," cried the chairman, "there must be something wrong here. You, Stokes, and you, Manning, and you, Bill Forbes, and you, William Blackmore, who seconded the resolution, all voted for it, of course, and now you vote against it. You can't vote two ways!"

Boot and shoemaker No. 2, with a white face, whispered something in a neighbour's ear, who thereupon said:

"Blackmore says he always votes on the contrary. He does it at home."

"But that can't be here," said the chairman; "we must all vote one way or the other. Are you in favour of this club?"

"Yes," every man cried.

"Is there any one not in favour of it?"

"No," every man cried.

"Then it's carried," said the chairman, "unanimously. Now we must give it a name."

Upon the face of every man present

dwelt a pondering expression, the general just interpretation of which would be vacuity. Half-a-dozen put their fingers to their brows, but not one of them had a name to propose.

The ever-ready chairman—and be it here remarked that Mr. Bartholomew was as good-humoured as he was apt—rose and said:

"It ain't the lightest of matters to give a fit name to such a club as ours. I think I can suggest one."

"Bart's the cleverest chap in the country," said one of the audience. "He ought to be Prime Minister."

Mr. Bartholomew resumed.

"I don't throw it in your teeth, mates; it's only a matter of reading, and I don't doubt in a year or two that some of you will know as much as me, and a good deal more. I don't throw it in your teeth, I say, that perhaps none of you ever heard the name of William Wilberforce."

They looked at each other, and shook their heads.

"He wasn't a working man, he was a gentleman with plenty of money; born a gentleman, and bred at college. But, mates, he was a man who saw things with a clear eye, and a clear heart that bled at the sight of oppression, and with a mind steadfast enough to accomplish what it was set upon. It is to William Wilberforce that we may say we owe—not only *we*, but all mankind—the abolition of slavery."

Tremendous applause.

"I don't know how many years this grand gentleman worked for it—worked and fought for it. He was beat over and over again in the House of Commons and the House of Lords, but he stuck to his guns, and on his death-bed he had the good news brought to him that the second reading of the Abolition of Slavery Bill was carried. He was a man, and every Englishman is proud of him. He was a man because he worked and fought on the side of humanity, and if any one here will propose that our club be called the 'Wilberforce Club' I don't think he could do a much better day's work."

Up jumped a dozen and proposed it, and the chairman conducted the question to an orderly issue. It was carried that the title of the institution should be the "Wilberforce Club." Then, pioneered by Mr. Bartholomew, other small matters of detail were discussed and settled. Present subscription of members, one penny per week, and the first week's subscription was paid into the hands of an elected treasurer. Sub-committees were appointed to form rules for the guidance of the club, and to look out for a suitable room in which to gather together. And then the meeting broke up, satisfied and gratified with the work it had done.

END OF VOL. II.

CHARLES DICKENS AND EVANS, CRYSTAL PALACE PRESS.

www.ingramcontent.com/pod-product-compliance
Lightning Source LLC
Chambersburg PA
CBHW032139230426
43672CB00011B/2386